Elijah Rawson

Articles on cases of intoxication related in the Christian Scriptures

Elijah Rawson

Articles on cases of intoxication related in the Christian Scriptures

ISBN/EAN: 9783337714765

Printed in Europe, USA, Canada, Australia, Japan

Cover: Foto ©ninafisch / pixelio.de

More available books at **www.hansebooks.com**

ARTICLES

ON

CASES OF INTOXICATION

RELATED IN THE

Christian Scriptures.

BY ELIJAH RAWSON.

AN ALUMNUS OF WHAT HAS BEEN CALLED "THE POOR BOYS' COLLEGE,"
[A PRINTING OFFICE]; FORMERLY EDITOR AND PUBLISHER OF THE
"YEOMAN'S RECORD" AT IRASBURGH, VT.; EX-PROFESSOR OF
TYPOGRAPHY, AND ASSISTANT-EDITOR IN SEVERAL NEWS-
PAPER OFFICES IN VERMONT AND NORTH-EASTERN NEW YORK.

ALSO

A SERMON BY BISHOP WELLES,
LATE BISHOP OF MILWAUKEE.

MILWAUKEE, WIS.
PRINTED BY THE RIVERSIDE PRINTING CO.
1889.

*Entered according to act of Congress in the year 1889, by
Elijah Rawson, in the office of the Librarian of
Congress at Washington.*

INDEX.

ARTICLE.		PAGE.
	Introduction	6
I.	Eve and Adam (Illustrated)	7
II.	Cain (Illustrated)	13
III.	Sons of God	17
IV.	Noah	21
V.	Inhabitants of a Plain in Shinar.	26
VI.	Abram	30
VII.	Lot	35
VIII.	Lot and His Daughters	43
IX.	Esau	47
X.	Rebecca and Jacob	51
XI.	Shechem, Dinah, Simeon and Levi	57
XII.	Joseph's Brethren	63
XIII.	Herod the Great, (2 illustrations).	68
XIV.	Herod Antipas	75
XV.	The Unthankful Subjects	79
XVI.	The Faithful Servant who may become an Evil Servant	89
XVII.	The Rich Young Man	96
XVIII.	The Two Sons	102
XIX.	The Wicked Husbandmen	108
XX.	The Unsympathetic Neighbors	115
XXI.	The Foolish Virgins	119
XXII.	The Wicked and Slothful Servant	123
XXIII.	Judas Iscariot, (Illustrated)	129
XXIV.	Peter, (Illustrated)	136
PORTRAIT of Bishop Welles		141
ECCLESIASTICAL Record of Bishop Welles		142
SERMON on the Prodigal Son, by Bishop Welles.		143

PREFACE.

SINCE coming to Milwaukee, several years ago, I have written several articles which have been published in "The Christian Statesman," under the general title of "CASES OF INTOXICATION RELATED IN THE SCRIPTURES." In those articles I used the word "Intoxication" in the large sense—including any influence which induces a person to do a wrong act, and in each article endeavored to show the connection between the cause of the act and the act and the consequences of the act, as gathered from the after history of the actors and their descendants, and added cautions and exhortations to the readers against the intoxicating influences of the world, the flesh and the devils; and also, in most cases, referring to a similar instance in the same volume.

Having on one occasion desired the opinion of the Rt. Rev. Dr. Welles, the late Bishop of Milwaukee, he kindly consented to examine one of the articles, and on expressing a favorable opinion of it, desired to examine the whole series as far as written, which he did, and as a result of that examination, expressed the opinion that they would be useful in a book-form.

In the following pages the full number of the articles as designed are presented, in the hope that they will help those who are struggling with the evil tendencies of their own hearts and the corrupting influences surrounding them, to maintain a successful contest against the foes of their well-being.

I do not claim that the subjects have been treated exhaustively, but I have tried to so present the leading thoughts and motives which may be drawn from the passages remarked upon, that readers of ordinary intelligence can understand what I have written, and by the aid of the Holy Spirit be enabled to keep themselves faithful and obedient servants of the Lord Jesus—The Christ.

I hereby acknowledge my obligations to Mr. Morehouse, of the Young Churchman Company, for the use of electrotypes with which this volume is illustrated.

E. R.

For testimonials see end of the volume.
405 Florida st., Milwaukee, Wis.

INTRODUCTION.

SO much has been said of the sin of Intoxication of late years, that the people of this generation have lost sight of the original cause of its first commission. When we wish to understand a subject thoroughly, it seems to me that we should look deeper into it than to merely consider the present manifestations of it, for it is not unlikely that, in the present day the beginnings of a course of inebriety may in many cases, be similar to that which caused the first occurrence of intoxication.

Alcohol is not the only thing that will cause intoxication; nor is that condition only caused by material things; for thoughts, fancies, and words, when accompanied by that mysterious influence known as animal magnetism, do intoxicate the human mind, so that those affected by them conduct themselves very differently from what they would were they not thus influenced.

I define intoxication to be that state of mind which leads a person to do or say what they would not do or say if they were fully aware of the results which would follow their conduct; such as when the passions are so excited that the individuals are beyond the control of reason.

I design, in the following pages to give some thoughts upon several of the Cases of Intoxication related in the Christian Scriptures, in the expectation that we may be able to discover the way in which the Lord dealt with those who, through the imperfection of their fallen nature were unable to resist the temptations which assailed them.

[I advise the reader in studying the subject to carefully read the passages of scriptures referred to.]

ARTICLE I.

Eve and Adam.—Gen. iii.

THE conduct of Eve, in her interview with the serpent, as related in the third chapter of Genesis, shows an evident excitement of feeling of the nature of intoxication. She was induced to consent to suggestions, which her love for her Creator and gratitude to her preserver and benefactor, would otherwise, in their unfallen state, have led her to reject with a decision and promptitude which would have rendered a repetition of the temptation not very likely to be offered. We may suppose that our first parents had not, at that time, discovered a process by which the juices of the fruits might be changed to an intoxicating liquid, or if they had, it is unreasonable to think that their natural taste had become so perverted that they would have relished such a beverage; therefore we will look in another direction for the cause of their intoxication.

The serpent, we are informed, was very subtle; and perhaps we can hardly form an idea of the cautious and wily movements with which he advanced in the process of temptation, the object of which was to seduce Eve and Adam from their cheerful and happy allegiance to God. It is probable that the first parts of the interviews are not given and that Satan had, by many previous acts and suggestions, prepared the way for the great skeptical question which was calculated to cast doubt upon God's word, and lead Eve to imagine that God really meant less than He said. Possibly Satan had sought first to influence her through the "lust of the flesh," calling her attention to the pleasurable sensations which the gratification of her appetite caused, advising her to a continued indulgence, when her natural judgment told her that her thoughts ought to be exercised by thankfulness to the Lord, and adoring admiration of His wonderful works spread around. Then the "lust of the eye" may have been addressed as he called to her notice the beauty of the fruit upon the tree in the midst of the garden, leading her to infer that its delicious qualities were as much superior to those of the other trees, as its inviting aspects were more attractive than the fruits from which she had hitherto supplied her real wants, so that, instead of raising her thoughts from its beauty to the power and wisdom of the Creator, she was drawn to thoughts of violating the only commandment which had been given them as a test of love and obedience by the Ruler of the Universe. And when the serpent assured her that the eating of the forbidden fruit would open her eyes, so that she would know good and evil by such a wonderful experience as would greatly increase her knowledge, her "pride of life" was powerfully appealed to, and she began to have imaginings similar to some modern ideas of progress; and so, instead of cheerfully waiting for such revelations as God might have been pleased to give in regard to the use which was to be made of the tree of knowledge of good and evil, she took and did eat.

After disobeying God herself, Eve sought her husband, taking with her some of the fruit and offered to him, which he, though probably aware of the source from which it was procured, and the strict command of the Creator relating to it, and to some extent the consequences which would result from an act of disobedience, ate of it, and thus became a partaker with her in the guilt and danger of the first transgression, influenced to the act by the fear of losing her companionship, unless he by sharing her guilt, should be able to share her punishment, which, so bewildered his mind, warped his judgment and excited his fears, that he was, like many of his descendants, induced to persevere in the gratification of a passion, though having good reason for believing that it would end in sorrow and irretrievable loss.

And they both soon found that shame, disgrace and condemnation was the result of yielding to the temptation; this being followed by expulsion from Eden, they realized by a bitter experience that for the gratification of a few sensual pleasures, they had lost the enduring delights of holiness and happiness in the ways of love and obedience, and entailed on themselves and their posterity, lives of labor, sorrow and pain in this life, with cause for fearful forebodings of still greater and more lasting distresses in a future state.

I think it may be stated that, as a general rule, the scriptures teach that all who pretend to have supernatural powers, except the accredited prophets and teachers of God's laws, are influenced by evil spirits, and therefore should be resisted and shunned. As a confirmation of this idea, I will refer to some passages in the bible bearing on the point. The first I refer to is in Lev. xix, 31, and in the same book [xx, 6, 27; Deut. xviii, 10—12]. And coming to the new testament, we have it stated as a fact that by Satan's influence Judas betrayed Christ. In the Acts of the Apostles we learn that Annanias and Sapphira were brought to ruin through the same influence.

In concluding I wish to give a few words of exhortation to the readers.

And first, I urge all, now that we have a way opened by which we may escape the fearful castrophe which the infatuation of our first parents has subjected their descendants, to look well to our surroundings and inward tendencies, and by the light of God's word, through the help of the Holy Spirit, and in the use of the providential means of grace, to avoid everything calculated to obscure in their minds the influence of the important truths that are intimately connected with their souls' welfare; and to suggest to them a few questions, which they can answer to themselves:

Do any perceive suggestions that seem to come from their own hearts which awake in them a desire to do or say something which their consciences convince them is displeasing to God? Parley not with the feeling, lest it prove a temptation of the devil, and they, like Eve, lament their yielding to his wiles, under a sense of the loss of purity, the favor of God, and their present and future happiness.

Do any imagine that sensual delights will compensate them for the neglect of the duties which are laid upon them to their Creator by their consciences? Put away the suspicious thought; lest they, like our first mother, find that what promises to be a delightsome gratification, turns upon them in a corroding remorse.

Do any have an idea come to their minds, that if they could be relieved of the restraints of the gospel, they would be happier now, and be able to better promote their own future happiness. Banish the false notion from their minds, lest they, like the first woman, discover that knowledge without holiness, will only render their souls more sensitive and miserable under the just condemnation of the most wise and powerful Being in the Universe, whose laws they have scorned, while living by His power, and enjoying the blessings of His providence.

Do any have thoughts that, if they could secure the approval of others to their notions of distrust of God's word, they would thereby acquire new strength to go on in the way of their fancies, and secure honor and applause among their fellow-men. Let them pause seriously before they try to attain such a result, lest they, like the first wife, learn by a sad and mortifying experience, that they have been doing that which will bring those they love to an inevitable and fearful destruction; and that instead of receiving plaudits and admiration, they receive imprecations accompanied by every imaginable manifestation of hate which the damned have power to express, and worse still, they feel that they deserve it; and, most dreadful of all, experience the righteous judgment of that Being whose wisdom they have foolishly imagined they could supplant by their impertinent folly.

Do any feel within themselves that they lack the moral power to withstand the allurements which are presented by their companions as they associate with them from time to time, and urge them to actions which they have reason to think will interfere with their duty, or by fostering in their minds a love for pleasures which are at variance with the holiness and purity of the gospel? Let them earnestly seek the assistance of the Holy Spirit to aid them in overcoming these temptations, lest they, like Adam, find that what they anticipated would afford them delight, after the short gratification of a few hours, turns upon them with remorseful upbraidings, which will embitter all their reflecting hours.

If any imagine that they can be successful in evading God's threatened punishments, by pleading as an excuse for the short-comings, that they were led into sin by the enticements of friends, or the influences which surrounded them; let them consider that God did not, in the case of our first father, hold such an excuse to be a sufficient one to exonerate him from blame, but visited upon him, not only the punishment of toil and labor for procuring bread and the temporal death of his body, but, unless he repented and had faith in that Seed of the woman who was to bruise serpent's head, will be visited with spiritual death at the day of judgment—which the scriptures represent to be "everlasting punishment" and "everlasting destruction from the presence of the Lord."

St. James said that if you "resist the devil he will flee from you," which you can do by the aid of the Holy Ghost, which will be given all who earnestly ask for it, and if you continue faithful unto death, you may at last be freely admitted to joys such as the human eye hath not seen, nor ear heard, neither have entered into the heart of the man to conceive—the things that God hath prepared for those that love Him —even Life Eternal.

ARTICLE II.

Cain.—Gen. iv.

THE account of the first person born on the earth—the second man of its inhabitants, is very meagre, but enough is given to indicate that he must have become intoxicated; but by what means we can only conjecture.

The first conjecture I make is that he was intoxicated by a false idea of his own importance, which was fostered by the treatment he received from his parents. It is noted that the great thought of his mother on the occasion of his birth was, that he was a gift from the Lord, and no doubt he was cherished as a most precious treasure, his parents making constant efforts to gratify every whim which his infantile, childish or youthful fancy conceived, which probably had the effect to create and confirm in his mind the idea that he was the most important person on the earth. And further to confirm this idea in Cain's mind, we find that on the birth of Abel, the parents thought so little of their second gift from the Lord, that they gave him a name which signified vanity, or a breath or vapor—and the reason may have been that he was a fragile infant,—not at all like the robust child—their eldest son, and they had little hope of his becoming anything that they would ever be proud of or receive pleasure from; and so in their treatment of the two brothers they made such a distinction between them as to make Cain feel that his pleasure was the main thing to be considered, and felt warranted in claiming and exercising that superiority which both his age and strength enabled him to enforce. And in his mature years we may suppose that he continued to

act on that principle in his dealings with his brother. This was, probably, the origin of the idea of the privileges of primogeniture; and by the 7th verse this principle seems to have been approved by the Lord, as Cain was plainly given authority over Abel, and was only blamed for the manner in which he exercised it. The brothers, it may be supposed, were trained up to worship God, as it appears to have been from a habit that they made the offerings hereafter alluded to, which were not the first sacrifices they had offered.

After living together for 127 years, in more or less of social intercourse, each in his particular department of labor—Cain in tilling the ground and Abel in keeping sheep—the conduct of Cain became so offensive to God that He would not accept his sacrifice, and from that circumstance arose that envious hate which resulted in the first murder and the first martyrdom of the world.

We may further imagine that the old tempter of Eve and Adam had not a little to do with this affair, and that his suggestions and enticements, not only to the parents that they need not be very strict with such young children, but also to Cain, which added to the natural and acquired habit of domineering over his brother, at last made successful the commission of this first fratricide.

Another conjecture may be hazarded. Although nothing is related in the scriptures to warrant a definite assertion of it as a fact, yet it does not appear unlikely that, in all those years, Cain might have discovered that the juices of the different fruits, when freed from the pulp made palatable drinks; that after remaining awhile became acrid, which, though at first not agreeable to his taste, in time, after many trials, at length became pleasant to him; and after a wearying time of labor afforded a reviving and stimulating draught, which produced in him a similar condition to the modern and more common kind of intoxication. Certainly there was much in his conduct and conversation which resemble the actions and words of a modern drunkard. But, however that may have been, it is very clear that he did what he would not have done, had he not in some way lost that control over himself that a virtuous man of mature age and experience may be expected to exercise—notice how he lied; how he imagined many sorts of troubles that he apprended would befall him; how he charged the Lord with injustice and cruelty; and eventually left the scene of his great crime in order to escape the continual reminder of his sins, and engaged in an enterprise which he doubtless intended to commemorate his own life on the earth, though he was wise enough to give it the name of his son rather than his own, which has ever since been regarded as a synonym for an overbearing, wicked and murderous character.

Of the children of Cain we have but little account in the first few generations, but we may suppose that they copied the example of the first murderer by allowing nothing but lack of power to stand between them and their wishes—each one ignoring all law and right, without regard to the wishes or welfare of others. We find the leading descendant of the sixth generation declaring that "if Cain shall be avenged sevenfold, truly Lamech seventy and sevenfold," [Gen. iv, 24,] which may indicate that he was of a revengeful disposition, and disposed to revenge himself to the greatest extent possible for any injury he might receive from others.

About 1,500 years later it is related that "the wickedness of man *was* great on the earth, and *that* every imagination of the thoughts of his heart *was* only evil continually," [Gen. vi, 5]; and for that reason God caused a flood which destroyed not only all of Cain's descendants, but all others who had been corrupted by their influence, so that only the family of Noah was worthy of of being preserved.

Cannot the readers who are parents find in the events above referred to, a lesson on the importance of training their children in such a way that they will not think of themselves "more highly than they ought to think?" [Rom. xii, 3.]

See another case: I. Sam. iii, 11—14; iv, 17—21.

And all who do not restrain their passions or indulge in an over-bearing behavior towards their associates, may find in this case a warning that they will be wise to heed, lest they, to use the very expressive simile of the scriptures, "Sow to the wind and reap the whirlwind." [Hosea viii, 7.]

The history of Saul, the first king of Israel, gives a pertinent example of the danger of cherishing such a habit of mind. [See references at end of Article xvii.

ARTICLE III.

THE SONS OF GOD.—Gen. vi.

THE 1st and 2d verses of this chapter state that "when men began to multiply on the face of the earth, and daughters were born unto them, that the sons of God saw the daughters of men, that they *were* fair, and they took them wives of all which they chose."

By men, in the 1st verse, is understood the descendants of Cain, who were brought up without religious training, and lived only for the world, and by the sons of God the descendants of Seth, who were religiously educated, and probably in some way brought into covenant relations with their Creator.

We may conclude that there were also daughters of God, who were more faithful in following the religious instructions of their parents than were the sons, even as it has been ever since ; that they were quiet, sedate and modest in their deportment, looking upon the affairs of this life as the events of a passage through a country to a better home ; and, perhaps, each one striving to make herself worthy of being the mother of the promised "seed of the woman" who should bruise the serpent's head.

But there were other women who behaved quite differently—who were active, lively and beautiful in forms and features, and every way calculated to produce a pleasing impression upon their youthful beholders. They were the daughters of men, who had not been instructed in religion, and were therefore only concerned about the affairs of this world—how to make a show and gain applause; how to win the affections of the opposite sex by arts and stratagems which should conceal the real sentiments of their hearts and the caprices of their conduct.

We may suppose that the descendants of Seth, during the first ages, were in the habit of being governed by the advice of their parents in all matters of importance —and the choice of a wife was then, as it should always be, regarded as the most important event of a man's worldly interests. [See Abraham's action in the matter of a wife for his son Isaac; and notice also the commands of God to parents in regard to their children's marriages. —Gen. xxiv, and Deut. vii, 3, 4.]

But in the progress of some 400 years, the young men began to imagine that they might safely choose for themselves, without consulting their parents, and so they "took them wives of all which they chose," from these irreligious, vain and crafty girls, thinking, perhaps, that they could, by their influence and authority over them, be able to induce them to love and obey the Lord; but they seem to have failed, if they had such ideas, for the balance of the influence was the other way—the young women were able to so influence their husbands, that they thought less of their religious duties and were less careful to train their children in the fear of the Lord. Evil spirits were busy on both sides—on the daughters of men to aid them in the practice of their arts to fascinate the young men, and on the sons of God to induce them to think that their parents had been too strict in their teachings and requirements; and so the chances were small that they would be able to maintain their religious character—thus they were exposed to assaults both in front and rear, which is as perilous a position for religious warriors, as for soldiers in earthly contests.

The 4th verse mentions two facts, one that "there were giants in the earth in those days." The most natural idea of this phrase is that they were men of extraordinarily large stature—whether such personages were then more common than they are now may be left to conjecture. In the opinion of some, they were not only great in their bodily development, but also great in wickedness—making great sensations by their cruel and impious exploits, and it may be that, from that source the childish idea of the later generations was derived, that giants were always cruel and blood-thirsty cannibals, whose presence was dreaded as much as the most ferocious and powerful wild beasts. The other fact, that the children of the sons of God by the daughters of men became " mighty men," and " men of renown." I imagine that, at that period much attention was given to the cultivation of the physical powers, and that the might and renown was somewhat like that which worldly people in these days accord to the pugilists, prize-fighters and pedestrians whose feats are chronicled with so much particularity by the secular newspapers, and read with such apparent interest by certain classes of our people.

But this state of things could not always last under such a Governor as the God of the Universe is represented to be in the bible, though He waited a hundred and twenty years before He executed the judgment upon them by the flood, which destroyed them all except the faithful Noah and his family.

The consideration of this subject in the light of the facts mentioned in the passages referred to, should teach young men the impolicy of making a choice of wives from those whose characters are not pure, and their conduct trifling and vain ; and young women the fearful risks they incur by accepting as husbands young men who are wanting in their duty to God or their fellowmen. Mere worldly riches and honors can never secure happiness in conjugal relations, and this fact is attested by the numerous applications for divorces which are made in this country. No man or woman is fully prepared to take upon themselves the duties of the marriage relation until they have become, in all sincerity children of God. The christian rule is: " Be ye not unequally yoked with unbelievers." [II. Cor. vi, 14.]

Another notable case was that of King Solomon, who in his prime indulged his fancies to the fullest extent; but who, in his old age wrote the results of his experience in those particulars in the 2d chapter of Ecclesiastes.

ARTICLE IV.

NOAH.—Gen. vi, 8, 9, and ix, 20—27.

BEFORE coming to the chief incident upon which I design mainly to write, I think it proper to recall to the reader the character of the man whose conduct is the theme of this article.

The 8th verse states that "Noah found grace in the eyes of the Lord." This expression seems to indicate that Noah was not an absolutely sinless man, but that he was so much imbued with human infirmity that he needed God's grace in order to make it consistent with the absolute purity and holiness of God's character, to regard him with complacence. But Noah was so earnest in his endeavors to overcome his imperfections, and was so resolute in withstanding the wicked influences that surrounded him, and so bold in reproving the ungodly deeds that he saw committed, and so faithful in warning his neighbors, and probably all with whom he had opportunity, of the fearful punishment impending over them unless they repented, and very likely, so humble and trustful in God's plan of overcoming the wiles of Satan that he was regarded by the Lord with favor. The phrase "perfect in his generations" may mean that, as compared with the others of his generation, he was so good that his imperfections were passed over. He endeavored to avoid everything sinful both in thought, word and deed, though, when withstanding the scoffs of his neighbors and the sight of their sinful doings, he must have given way to thoughts, if not to words and actions which showed that his soul was vexed at their wicked deeds, and indicated that he lacked that full confidence in God, which is an important attribute of a perfectly holy man. The phrase "Noah walked with God" in the 9th verse probably means that he was careful to regulate his life agreeably to God's will, and that he sought to learn that will by much meditation and prayer, and we have evidence that God approved and answered his prayer.

The 20th verse of the 9th chapter states that "Noah began to be a husbandman." For the last hundred years he had been so busy in building the ark that he had little time to attend to the cultivation of the ground, and probably lived on such fruits as grew without cultivation, and the milk and the flesh of animals. But now he had leisure to do something in the way of cultivating crops (and, perhaps the climate on the mountains of Ararat was such that cultivation was necessary to secure sufficient supply of food.) At any rate it may be fairly supposed that he saw that it was important both for their happiness and integrity, that he and his sons should be employed in some useful occupation; and it may be stated that the lack of a necessity for a moderate amount of labor may have been one great cause of the wickedness before the flood. It appears that, besides the cultivation of the crops needed for food, he also planted a vineyard. The 21st verse contains the first statement of the manufacture of wine, but does not speak of it in such a way as to indicate that it was a new discovery. The latter part of the verse shows that Noah had not been accustomed to its use. I am inclined to think that in planting the vineyard, the making of wine and in using it, he was only trying experiments; and we may suppose that the last experiment was never repeated by him. Considering the circumstances, we may not blame Noah in this affair; but there are some further circumstances about the case which should be studied with care.

The honor and respect paid to parents has been, in all ages, a distinguishing mark of the good; next in importance to our duty to our Creator, is our duty to our father and mother, and no doubt Noah had carefully trained his children in a proper reverence for their superiors, and was not disposed to overlook any want of a proper respect on their part, toward God or himself or his wife, and when so flagrant an act of disrespect as is related in the 22d verse, was brought clearly to his attention, his sense of duty to his sons made him resolve to do what he could to prevent a repetition of the act, therefore, he, after having ascertained all the circumstances, pronounced the curse and the blessings related in the 25th, 26th and 27th verses. And we may say that the curse was not pronounced because it was the real desire of Noah that Canaan should suffer undue punishment, but he saw that the tendency of the act, if left unrebuked, would be that his descendants would relapse into the wicked habits which had prevailed before the flood, and for that reason he felt it his duty to manifest his displeasure.

It will be perceived that the act which is mentioned as displeasing Noah was performed by Ham, and that the curse was pronounced upon Canaan, who was Ham's youngest son; he in the 24th verse is styled Noah's younger son, from which it may be inferred that Moses considered grandchildren as also the children of a man. [See Gen. xxi, 43.] Ham was Noah's second son—at least it may be so inferred from the order in which their names are mentioned. I am inclined to believe that Canaan first made the discovery and told his father, when Ham, instead of showing the respect that his brothers did to Noah went and saw his nakedness and reported it to Shem and Japhet in a sportive way, and thus incurred the just displeasure of the greatest man upon the earth at that time.

It may be considered a question whether Noah's declarations in the 25th, 26th and 27th verses are a prophecy, or only a sentence which he pronounced as his decision of what the sin deserved; and also, whether God carried out the sentence in the further ordering of His providence. I believe that nothing further is recorded of the after history of Canaan except the naming of his descendants And it also may be considered a question whether the curse pronounced against Canaan was intended to be visited upon his descendants. Canaan's decendants settled in Palestine, and were powerful and wicked peoples when the Israelites destroyed them, excepting the inhabitants of Gibeon, who by craft secured a league by which their lives were spared; but for their deception were made hewers of wood and drawers of water to the congregation. [See Josh. chap. ix.] And other descendants of Ham, who settled in Egypt, became a very learned and prosperous people, who made slaves of the Children of Israel. I am inclined to think that the curse related only to Canaan himself. The later generations of the Canaanites were punished for their own sins; and the blessings were for Shem and Japhet themselves and their descendants who were virtuous, but were forfeited by those who were vicious.

The great sin brought to view in this article is the dishonoring of parents, and the lesson to be enforced from it is one which there seems to be great need of heeding in these later times; and I would endeavor to impress upon the minds of all children of religious parents the duty of regulating their lives by the instructions which they receive from their fathers and mothers, and in general of all parents whose commands do not contravene the laws of God.

Another scriptural case of dishonoring parents is found in the account of Absalom, recorded in the xv, xvi, xvii and xviii chapters of 2d Samuel.

Christ's instructions on the subject of honoring parents may be learned from Matthew xv, 5—7.

ARTICLE V.

INHABITANTS OF A PLAIN IN SHINAR.—Genesis xi, 1—9.

AMONG the many emotions which disturb the minds of the people of the earth, there is, perhaps, none more prevalent than that of discontent with present circumstances, and one which Christians are exhorted against when they are taught that they should "be contented and do their duty in that state of life in which it pleases God to call" them; and which St. Paul declared that he had learned, though he was naturally of a very impetuous disposition, [See Phil. iv, 11—12.] With the majority of people this feeling is so overpowering that they cannot really enjoy their present comforts, because some fancied pleasures are beyond their reach, or through fear that the blessings which are present will not be continued to them, but be followed by less desirable circumstances. It is doubtless true that all would be happier, and be able to do more to secure the happiness of others, could they banish from their minds the fearful anticipations of evil to come, which destroy present enjoyments, mar future hopes, and are sources of vain desires, which often harass them with disappointments.

The first nine verses of the 11th chapter of Genesis contain a remarkable exhibition of this feeling—that may be a sort of intoxication.

The first verse of the passage states that at that time (about 100 years after the flood,) " the whole earth was of one language," and had the people been content to have used it in expressions of gratitude to God, and good will to each other, it might have continued to the present time, and thus rendered unnecessary those dreams of philologists respecting the perfecting of the languages, and ideas of inventing one which all nations would be willing to accept and use (discarding their ancestral tongues), thus making the spread of light and knowledge more rapid and easy.

But the people of this plain had some new ideas,— instead of continuing to cultivate their lands and enjoy the fruits, they seemed possessed of a public spirit —a desire to do something famous, without reference to the will of God, one of their propositions being, in fact, an attempt to provide a place of safety in case another inundation should be sent upon the earth, although God had made a special promise to Noah that He would not again destroy the people of the earth by a flood. Under the circumstances the proposition, and the actions for carrying it into effect, were nothing short of an insult to the Lord. They said: . . . . " let us make brick;" they were not content with ordinary wood dwellings, or with sun-dried brick homes, but they would have them " burnt thoroughly" so that it might be an indestructible material which would be less liable to the danger of conflagrations, and would be likely to remain for the occupancy of their descendants, who would thereby be reminded of what had been done for them by their ancestors; nor were they content with the scattered dwellings of agriculturists, but wished them built compactly, so that they could have the benefit of a society, and an organized system of protection against the many dangers which the scattered dwellers on farms were liable; and further, they would have a " tower whose top *may reach* unto heaven" —that it might be seen at great distances so as to excite the wonder and curiosity of those who should come near enough to get a view of its elevated summit, and who on coming nearer, would be more and more astonished at the magnificent design, the lofty structure and the wonderful concentration of labor necessary in order to accomplish such a vast enterprise,—and then, when the pilgrims should return to their own homes, they could tell of the great things they had seen on a plain in Shinar, and thus the fame of their doings would be spread wherever mankind had made a habitation—and they would make themselves "a name."

This, they imagined, would prevent them from being "scattered abroad from the face of the whole earth." But all these plans were conceived and attempted to be carried out without reference to the will of the Lord, and, as we have noticed before, in a distrust of His promise, and in this fact we see a reason for His interfering to punish their impiety by disappointing their ambition, and exhibiting His power to frustrate their schemes—or, perhaps, He only withheld His providential assistance to keep them in the normal use of their faculties, making them like a community of lunatics, unable to understand each other, or to form any feasible plans for the prosecution of their public interests. And "thus the Lord scattered them abroad from thence upon the face of the earth."

What might be said of the future history of Babel will not be attempted in this article, except to refer the reader to the book of Daniel, (chapter i—v,) which relates the leading events of the last eighty years of the Babylonish nation (during the reigns of its two last kings,) and proves that the same proud and impious spirit actuated the descendants of those people of the plain of Shinar who remained in the place where the confusion of language occurred, as shown by their ancestors 1,700 years before, and also tells the different ways in which the Lord punished their impiety.

We are taught by the incidents related in this history, that it is unwise to form plans and attempt to carry them out, which ignore the overruling providence of God, or which imply a distrust in His promises; and they are wisest who choose as the rule of their conduct the revealed will of the Lord.

To the young I would particularly recommend to be guided by the advice of their religious elders, whose experience and judgment qualify them to give direction to the inexperienced.

I close this article by advising all "who profess and call themselves christians," that they, in all the vicissitudes of life, seek through prayer the direction of the Holy Spirit, as the best means by which they can expect to be guided into the most important truths, and thus learn by experience the way of true happiness and prosperity.

ARTICLE VI.

Abram—Gen. xii, 11—20.

IN the 31st verse of the 11th chapter of Genesis is the first mention of Abram, who afterwards became the most famous religious man the civilized world has ever known; and although I mainly design in this article to notice an indiscreet act, on his part, (which indicates that we are not to expect to find "a just man upon earth, that doeth good and sinneth not,"—Eccl. vii, 20), yet it may be profitable to bear in mind some of the incidents of his life previous to the events to which I particularly invite the readers' consideration. In this passage it is stated that, though a married man, he was still a member of his father's family, and under that parent's control, until Terah's death, as mentioned in the next verse.

After his father's death Abram received a communication from the Lord directing him to leave the place where he was dwelling and go to a land which would be shown him, and God gave him great promises, which were to be fulfilled to his descendants mainly, though he himself was to receive abundant blessings, among which was the very satisfactory one that he should "be a blessing" to others, even to "all the families of the earth." [See chap. xii, 1—3.]

Abram, agreeable to this command and with faith in these promises, departed out of Haran, and when he and his family had reached Canaan and passed through considerable portions of it, the Lord made known to him that that was the land which he had given to his "seed"; and in token of his acquiescence in this

ABRAM. 31

decision Abram built an altar unto the Lord, and that appears to have been his usual practice wherever he sojourned. [See verses 5—9.]

The 10th verse mentions that a grievous famine afflicted the land, and that, for that reason he went down into Egypt to remain there until better times should come, no doubt intending to return when fruitful seasons should again be restored. It may be properly supposed that this famine was visited upon the land as a punishment for the wickedness of the people thereof, that being one of the ways, which the bible declares, that God punishes those who disobey His commands.

I now come to the 11th verse which gives the first account of Abram's departure from the truth, or rather keeping back an important fact, in his dealings with the king of Egypt.

From the fear that the Egyptians would become so enamored with the beauty of his wife that they would kill him for the sake of obtaining her, he directed her to say that she was his sister, and not to tell the further important fact that she was his wife.

Some scholars affirm that, at that time (not far from 325 years after the confounding of the language at Babel) the word sister had a wider signification than we now confine it to—the same as Lot was called Abram's brother in the xiv c. and 16th v., when he was only his nephew, according to our reckoning. In the xx c. v. 12, Abram is represented as saying that Sarah was the daughter of his father, but not the daughter of his mother, possibly meaning that she was the granddaughter of his father. In that large sense he may have correctly called her his sister; but in the plot which he formed with her, he intended to deceive the Egyptians, and that constituted his sin.

The 14th and 15th verses give the result of the plot upon the Egyptians, upon the king's household and upon the king. The people admired her, the princes praised her, and the king took measures to make her his wife; and on Abram he bestowed favors, giving him the means of living in princely style that he might be qualified to associate with royalty. But trouble came of it; the Lord would not permit Abram to lose his wife in that way, even though it was caused by his own fault. The 17th verse states that "the Lord plagued Pharaoh and his house with great plagues because of Sarai, Abram's wife." The reason why Pharaoh and his family were punished in this instance, instead of Abram is not made known, but we may be sure that in some way it was deserved; and we may perceive that the Lord did not visit upon Abram the full consequences of his sin, and we will suppose, as one reason, that it was because he was really suspicious that the Egyptians were so wicked that they would not hesitate to take his life if they knew that Sarai was his wife. Another reason will be found in the promises God had made to Abram which would seem to have failed had he been a great sufferer in his intercourse with those among whom he sojourned; but had he been fully awake to the faithfulness of the Lord to the promises he had received, it would have saved him from the temptation of resorting to deception to save himself from harm.

The 17th, 18th and 19th verses contain the account of the interview between Pharaoh and Abram, in which the latter is called to answer for his duplicity. He makes no reply, thus seeming to acknowledge his guilt, and no doubt felt that he had been unwarrantably suspicious of the Egyptians, though there may be reasons for believing that if they had not suffered punishments from God, and had not feared more of them, they would not have treated Abram so leniently.

By the 20th verse we learn that the king sent Abram away in a friendly spirit, probably fearing to displease one who was so unmistakably under the protection of a power above human control.

The lessons which these incidents should teach the people of God is: 1st, that they should be truthful in their dealings, and particularly, not to deceive by concealing any important fact in relation to matters about which they are dealing; 2d, that they should put their trust in God amidst all their difficulties, and not doubt but that He will make their trials result in their best good, if they are truthful, obedient and humble; 3d, that if, through temptation or fear they do come short of their duty, God will overlook their short-comings, if they truly repent and renew their diligence in striving to avoid them in the future; 4th, that they should not be censorious or captious when they see failings in others, but remember that the best of Christians have failings, and when they pray to be delivered from evil, let their thoughts especially include all whose sins have particularly affected or interested them; and 5th, that they should be careful to avoid all appearance of evil, lest the opposers of religion find occasion, through the unfaithfulness or timidity of their lives, to speak against the cause of Christ, and so endanger their own souls and the souls of those who are under their influence.

For other cases mentioned in the Bible of the same fault, see chap. xx, where Abram committed it again, under similar circumstances, with similar results; also chap. xxvi, 7—11 verses, tells how Isaac did the same thing at Gerah, and for the same reason.

St. Paul very forcibly teaches what should be a

Christian's course on this point in his epistle to the Ephesians, iv, 14, 15; "That we *henceforth* be no more children, tossed to and fro, and carried about with every wind of doctrine, by the sleight of men, *and* cunning craftiness, whereby they lay in wait to deceive; but speaking the truth in love, may grow up into him in all things, which is the head, *even* Christ."

ARTICLE VII.

Lot.—Genesis xiii, 8—13; xiv, 8—16; xix, 1—26.

LOT and Abram were both good men, and in the best sense of the word "gentlemen," who wished to be at peace with each other, and have all about them peaceful. But their flocks and herds were so great, which required so many employes to look to and manage, and the conflicting interests of the two masters, were taken so much to heart by the two sets of herdmen, that they could not well avoid contention, so that Abram made the proposition that they should separate, and gave to Lot his choice of the way he would go, while Abram would take the opposite direction. It does not appear that Lot had any hesitation as to his choice, or that he asked Abram's advice, but that he was only guided by what appeared to be most for his worldly advantage, seeming to ignore the possibility that there might be something in the character and habits of the people of the place where he should locate which would render them undesirable neighbors. Whether Lot understood the character of the people of Sodom before he went there may be doubted, but he soon had an experience, which must have convinced him that he had made a serious mistake, for there appeared armed hosts in the vicinity of Sodom, who made the possession of life and property very precarious,—the forces of nine kings were joined in battle, and the city of Sodom captured, its goods and provisions taken, and Lot was taken captive, and would probably have been made a slave had not Abram by remarkable acts of strategy delivered him and recaptured the goods of Sodom.

For the space of nine years the book of Genesis relates nothing more of Lot; but St. Peter [II Pet. ii, 7, 8,) says that just Lot was "vexed with the filthy conversation of the wicked; for that righteous man dwelling among them, [the people at Sodom] in seeing and hearing, vexed his righteous soul from day to day with their unlawful deeds." Why he should have remained among such people is most easily explained by imagining that he had a missionary spirit which moved him to labor and hope that he might prevail upon those wicked people to change their vile courses of life and become obedient to the laws of God. But we have no evidence that he met with any success in such efforts—there does not appear to have been one righteous man besides Lot, for had there been any, it was most probable that they would have escaped with him.

In pursuing the history of Lot, we learn by the 19th chapter that one evening two angels approached the gate of Sodom, where Lot was sitting, and, as was probably his custom when strangers of gentle-seeming came near him, he rose to meet them and offered them the hospitalities of his house, which they at first declined, but finally accepted, after which their host prepared for them a sumptuous feast of which they partook. On observing the unusual festivity in Lot's house, his wicked neighbors, suspicious of something that might occur from the interviews of the strangers with their reprover, or, perhaps chagrined because they had not been invited to share the feast, surrounded the house and demanded that Lot should bring out his guests to them that they might ascertain who they were and what was the reason of their visit; and when their demand was denied by Lot, who remonstrated with them for their incivility, they made riotous demonstrations which they were only prevented from carrying into effect by a miraculous interposition in behalf of Lot and his family.

The next morning the angels hurried Lot and his family away from Sodom, and guided them to a place of safety (except Lot's wife, who by disobeying the orders of the rescuers, was changed into a pillar of salt.) But after the terrible destruction of the cities of the plain Lot was afraid to remain even in Zoar, choosing rather to brave the dangers of the mountain than to remain among the wicked people of that little city. And so he, with his two daughters, dwelt in a cave in the mountain, with but a precarious supply of food and only such conveniences for comfort as they had been able to bring with them by hand. It must have seemed to him a very sorry change; for he had been accustomed for many years, with his numerous flocks and herds, to generous supplies of the delicacies of that generation. But this was not the worst of it.

Instead of being able to reform any of the inhabitants of Sodom, the inroads of wickedness were made upon Lot's family; some of his daughters had married inhabitants of the city and were, doubtless, partakers of the wickedness as well as sharers in its destruction; and even his wife's fate was scarcely less severe.

It may be profitable to inquire the cause of this wickedness of the people of the plain. The account informs us that it was a very fertile country, and those who lived there could gain a subsistence with little labor or care, and therefore had much leisure; and when such is the case the natural tendency of mankind is to corrupt each other by vain and sinful amusements which lower the standard of morality and virtue, unless counteracted by a preponderating religious or moral influence, which Lot in his destitution of religious sympathy could not furnish, though had he had the assistance of ten righteous men, they possibly might have been able to withstand the current of evil and made progress in saving some of the people from the prevailing vices; at least they would have secured a further time of probation for their fellow citizens.

It is better for the morals and manners of a community that its individuals should be under the necessity of spending the most part of each day in some regular employment—something besides mere pass-time—something permanently useful to themselves or others. And therefore it is, that among those peoples whose necessities are supplied by a small amount of care and labor, their mental faculties are dwarfed, and their bodies enervated, and their social condition but little better than that of brutes.

I add other paragraphs, which are written from the stand-point of a conservative New Englander, who never was afflicted with the Western fever, but, whose family being scattered, is making a several month's visit to the family of a daughter who has been a resident of the West more than a score of years. I doubt the wisdom, in many cases, of persons who have left a comfortable property in the East and came West. They may have improved their worldly circumstances, been able to live with less labor, and indulge themselves and families with more luxuries; but this temporal improvement has been accompanied by influences tending to make them think less of those moral and religious truths and duties which are the foundations of a happy and prosperous condition in a community, and also foster in their minds a love for amusements which are of a questionable character, thus undermining that religious sense which would lead them to take delight in the ways of God's commandments and in seeking his blessing, without which worldly riches will be likely to prove a curse which will grow heavier as the generations pass, till they end in a state of society as much to be deplored as was that of Sodom in the days of Lot. And some, too, who were not possessors of real estate or the proprietors of a flourishing business might with prudence have remained in the East, and worked themselves gradually to a competence, instead of leaving their parents in loneliness in their old age to long for their cherished one, or give up their old home and follow a son or a daughter to new scenes that would be likely to impair their quiet and comfort in their declining years; they may not have so quickly attained that competence, and probably would never have been subjected to the dangers and responsibilities of the rich, but they might have as effectually served their generation, enjoyed the comforts of this life and secured God's favor, and so have been prepared to enter and enjoy the rest that remaineth for the people of God, in Paradise, after the struggles and trials of this transient life are over. The effect of the free emigration from the Eastern States has been to retard their progress in becoming what the pioneers in those parts hoped and labored for —a cultivated, comfortable and conscientious people. Particularly in the agricultural districts, where small farmers having sold out to large farmers, have left a decreasing population, so that the poorer people have not so good a chance for the education of their children as was enjoyed a generation ago; Christian churches have died out, or continue in a feeble and discouraged condition, giving reasons for sad forebodings as to the future; and all kinds of business has become dull from scarcity of well-to-do people to exchange labor and products with each other. It is not quite so bad in the larger towns and villages, but even there business is less thriving than it would have been had an energetic class of farmers continued to cultivate and improve their small farms as they might have done, thus giving patronage to various mechanics who would have been encouraged to remain and help on the general prosperity.

May not the people of the Near-West make some profitable use of these thoughts when the idea comes to them of going to the Far-West; as I perceive indications that a spirit of discontent with present prospects is at work in the minds of some of its people, which may result in an emigration from the deteriorated and high-priced lands of this region to the fresh and cheap lands of the newer settlements, and thus re-enact in some degree that condition of things which has kept the New England States from the full realization of what they might have been had a fair proportion of her young people remained to improve her farms, and become the fathers and mothers of moral and religious descendants, whose rules of life were drawn from the bible, and whose chief object would have been "to glorify God and enjoy Him forever."

I do not expect that all the children of a large family will remain at or near the old homestead, though there are but few parents but would be gratified to have their children settle near them; but I think it not too much to hope that at least one of a christian family of children should consider it a religious duty to remain in the locality hallowed by their birth and early experiences; and if done with the motive of cheering and comforting their parents in their declining years, I doubt not that the blessing of God would attend such a course; and with such a plan carried out, no portion of our country that has a healthy climate, would fall into decay, but would gradually improve, both temporally and spiritually, till it would be recognized as like unto the "garden of the Lord."

In these thoughts I have not lost sight of the fact that God calls some of his children to preach the gospel, and others by some strong bent of inclination or genius, to a different course of life from that of their parents; but in such cases I should hope that their motives would be free from selfish ambitions, and prompted by a sense of duty to God, remembering the truth which St. Paul taught the Corinthians, that "the things which are seen *are* temporal; but the things which are not seen *are* eternal." [II Cor. iv, 18]; and do not forget the instruction which Jesus gave to his disciples [Matt. vi, 33]: "Seek ye first the kingdom of God and His righteousness and all these things [food, drink and clothing] shall be added unto you."

Not only has this vast emigration been bad for the Eastern States, but has been so for the Nation. First, by encouraging a spirit of speculation, or a disposition to gain sudden wealth by means of buying large tracts of land, and then by holding them for a great advance in price, and by skillful management gain riches without earning them; and in doing this they stood in the way of actual settlers gaining homesteads in desirable locations, obliging them to go farther into the unexplored territory, while at the same time, in most cases, these operations tended to lower the morals of the speculators, if not peril their souls. Second, by giving strong inducements to reckless individuals to violate the laws which were intended to secure the faithful performance of the terms of our treaties with the Indians, which has offended these aboriginal owners of the country, giving them just cause for their hostilities against those who had the temerity to infringe upon the rights which had been promised them by solemn treaties, which infringements have been the cause of numerous wars that have cost the nation untold treasure, great hardships and unnumbered lives; and has also retarded the civilization and christianization of the Indian people; besides being the occasion of the lapsing into almost the condition of barbarism, of numerous descendants of European races.

AN EXPLANATION.

I omit a discussion of Abraham's second dissimulation respecting Sarah's relation to him (the names of Abram and Sarai having both been changed,) contained in the 20th chapter of Genesis, verses 2—18, only remarking that the repeating of the prevarication, by so good a man, when he had been so emphatically reproved over 20 years before, may be explained by considering that the circumstances of the occasion may have been of a nature to appear more threatening than those of the first occasion; and that, possibly, may have been the cause of his second attempt to deceive. By these incidents in the life of the man who became one of the most celebrated characters among those whose lives are recorded in the bible, (excepting Jesus of Nazareth,) as well as a similar incident in the life of his son Isaac, of whom the fewest imperfections are mentioned of any human biblical character, (Gen. xxvi, 7—11,) we are led to the belief that no descendant of the first Adam ever has or ever will attain perfection in this life, and can, therefore, be admitted to the holy society of the heavenly state only through the merits of the second Adam, and by the help of the Holy Ghost.

ARTICLE VIII.

LOT AND HIS DAUGHTERS.—Gen. xix, 30—38.

IN the passage noted above we have an account of circumstances attending a case of intoxication, which is regarded, even by those who are disposed to look upon drunkenness as a sin of light degree, as one of peculiar guilt, not indeed as rendering the drunken person guilty, but as making him an object of pity—but they who by wiles accomplish that object deserve reprobation. And when persons are enticed by stratagem to submit to be brought to such a state of insensibility that they are unaware of what they do or what is done with them, we can scarcely blame them; and yet we cannot but think them censurable for becoming the dupes of the designing, who seek by covert means to procure what could not be obtained by fair and open dealing.

The conduct of Lot's daughters in their conspiracy against their father, to our ideas and in our times, seems very wicked, but to them, in their peculiar circumstances, it may not have appeared so very sinful, though they had, doubtless, been instructed that such behavior, under ordinary circumstances, was highly improper, as may be inferred from the necessity of getting their father into a state of mental bewilderment before they could hope to succeed in their scheme. As this passage is the last historical mention of Lot, it is probable that he died soon after, a disappointed man as far as worldly prosperity was concerned ; and it may be doubted whether he knew of the disgraceful conduct of his daughters.

Lest we judge these young women too harshly let us endeavor to imagine the peculiar circumstances in which they were placed. First, they were women, with the natural propensities of that sex, a prominent one of which is, when not overshadowed by the delusions of irreligious fashions, a desire for children and a delight in the care of them. Witness the joy and assiduity with which little girls attend upon their dolls, and the patience and self-sacrifice they exhibit in caring for a real baby, or for their younger brothers and sisters. I think it is clearly a divinely appointed destiny for women both to bear and care for children, and when these functions are performed in accordance with the dictates of religion, they are attending to their highest earthly duties. Second, consider their issolation; they believed that their father was the only person with whom they were ever likely to meet with, and so, as the only means by which they could gratify their motherly instincts, they had recourse to stratagem; but in doing this, they violated the plainest dictates of filial duty, the precepts of religion and the innate modesty of their sex. It appears evident, too, from their conduct, that they had become contaminated with the vile ideas of the inhabitants of Sodom, and therefore were disposed to look on their sinful actions as not so very bad; they regarded their father as righteous over-much, and thought his teachings too strict, and so cast them aside as the rules of their own lives.

In imagination we may follow them to the results of their actions into motherhood. They saw their infant children, and doubtless rejoiced in their possession, and probably never were so happy as when ministering to their infantile wants, and watching the progress of the development of their opening faculties and the increase of their physical powers.

But time passed on; the boys became youths, and very probably, as they were the only children of their mothers, were very willful, and as children so situated are likely to be the ruling members of their families—especially if their fathers are not among the number—we may readily suppose that the boys were often quarrelsome, and the sisters each naturally caring most for her own son, they must for that reason, often appeared to each other as unfriendly. It may fairly be inferred that but a small amount of true enjoyment was the lot of the little community.

And when these youths became men were they a source of pleasure? We may easily suppose that a true mother, in no period of her life experiences more satisfaction in her own children than when, if they become habituated to right principles and conduct, she sees them taking their places in the world's activities and exhibiting those qualities of mind and heart which she has endeavored to foster in them, and habits which show that correct principles have taken firm root in their characters; and, on the contrary, when a woman of devout religious affections sees in the conduct of her children when at mature age, evidences that they fear not God nor regard man (even to the degree of not honoring their father and mother,) she cannot but have fearful forebodings both for their spiritual and temporal welfare. It is morally certain that these daughters of Lot could have had little or no satisfaction in the conduct of their sons when they became men; for judging from the character of their descendants we may suppose that they were willful and stubborn, caring little for their mothers, or for the will of God as it had been taught by their grandfather-father Lot.

The 37th verse states that the eldest woman named her son Moab, and that he was the father of the nation of the Moabites, whose king 445 years later refused to allow the children of Israel to pass through their country on the way to the land of Canaan; and endeavored through the prophet Balaam to bring God's curse upon them, but was signally defeated in his attempts; and during a long period of the history of Israel the Moabites were the cause of great afflictions and terrors and sins to the chosen people of God, till at last, about 400 years after their settlement in the land promised to Abraham, they were subdued by David. [See Numbers xxiii; xxiv; xxxi; and II. Samuel viii, 2.

The youngest woman's son was named Ben-ammi, and his descendants formed the nation of the Ammonites. They were wicked and idolatrous, and in many ways caused trouble and distress to God's people. About 750 years after the birth of Ben-ammi the Ammonites were subdued by Israel's famous general, Jepthah, the account of which is given in the 11th chapter of Judges.

Another case where an attempt was made to secure a selfish object and cover a grievous wrong by procuring intoxication, was the affair of David with Uriah [see II. Sam. xi]; but the soldierly bearing and patriotic devotion of Uriah frustrated the plan of the king, and he was induced to do what in the sight of the Lord was the same as murder, by conspiring for the death of the veteran soldier, with a view of covering his sin; but it was not covered, as it is still known as the greatest blot on the character of that man who in most respects was a model of a general and statesman, a poet and devout worshiper of the true God. But God would not allow his sin to go unpunished, therefore the child was not permitted to live, but was taken from his grief-stricken parents; and the case yet remains a warning that God will not permit, even His most favored servants, to sin against Him with impunity.

ARTICLE IX.

Esau—Genesis xxv, 29—34.

ISAAC'S eldest son seems to have borne a similar relation in his father's family that Cain did in the family of Adam—that of an energetic and passionate man who was subject to caprices, and also being of a wild disposition, which made him rather disagreeable to his mother, though his father admired his skill in hunting, and probably had great hopes of his future success from the energy he displayed in his chosen course of life; but his case, as well as most cases of individual history since that time, shows that a predilection for the chase is not favorable to the formation of a religious character, or a firm and self-reliant disposition of any kind; while the wanton cruelty which it fosters in the heart is opposed to every humane impulse of a benevolent mind. And further, the habit of relying upon a chance supply of materials for food, rather than by prudent forethought and steady labor according to a well-considered plan, is conducive to vacillating habits both of thought and action, which unfit the mind for such consecutive thought as is necessary for apprehending religious and moral truths, which is an important aid to a proper understanding of our duties both to God and man, or for such constant and well-directed efforts as are likely to be successful in securing temporal comfort and prosperity.

And it came to pass that, notwithstanding Esau's skill in hunting, there was a time when it did not avail to supply him with what was necessary to sustain life, and he returned to the home faint, weary, and so disheartened that he thought he was about to die. With great importunity he asks his brother for some of the red pottage which he had been preparing; but Jacob declined to give it without remuneration—something which should compensate him for his labor in procuring the materials and preparing them for use. The vegetable called lentiles is supposed to have produced fruit resembling some varieties of modern beans and peas, therefore from them Jacob was able to furnish a very satisfying repast for a hungry man, he probably having been accustomed to assist his mother in her domestic labors, as she had no daughters to take a share in such employments, and it was no doubt his helpfulness in this particular which made him so much a favorite with Rebecca.

Jacob, on Esau's request for food, asked his brother to sell him his birthright, and Esau seemed to acquiesce without hesitation. But Jacob was not satisfied with a mere casual assent, but required a solemn oath on the subject, and the other, with apparently no reflection, gave the asservation demanded, and then partook of the food given him, and thoughtlessly went his way, little thinking of the importance of the concession he had made to his brother. But some forty years afterwards [see chap. xxvii., v. 34—41] he bitterly regretted his conduct on this occasion, but could get no change of his father's decision, and he was so exasperated at the result that he wickedly contemplated murdering his brother.

Many scripture expounders think Jacob was to blame for his conduct on this occasion, but, perhaps, the most that can be said is that he exhibited a lack of brotherly affection. We do not know what provocations he may have had. In their childhood and youth, probably, they had many disagreements and quarrels, owing to their widely differing temperaments, and in them we may suppose that Esau was overbearing and tyrannical, compelling Jacob to give up to him on occasions of differences in choice of amusements or occupations, and this state of things tended to make the younger brother disposed to take measures at every convenient opportunity to get an advantage of his elder brother. As they were twins the difference in their ages was but a trifle, and it must have been rather galling to Jacob to be expected to give up to one who was so little his senior. It is not unlikely, also, that Rebecca may have informed her youngest son of the Lord's appointment in regard to him [see v. 23,] and as he was at that time between thirty and forty years old, he thought it time to claim the privileges which that appointment implied, and so took this method of getting an acknowledgment of them from his elder brother.

The privileges to which Esau was entitled by reason of his being the first-born son were that, on his father's death, he would have received a double portion of his father's wealth, become the priest of the family, and when the descendants of Isaac became numerous, be the chief of the tribe; and if they had become a nation, his eldest son or other eldest son of an eldest son would have been the king. These were what he sold to Jacob for a mess of pottage.

By the laws of Moses the eldest son was to receive a double portion of the estate, and on him devolved the duty of maintaining the honor and credit of the family, after the father's death, and probably the support of the widowed mother or stepmother, if there was one.

The superiority of position and influence which, in most civilized nations, is accorded to the eldest child of a family (particularly if a son) finds its reasonableness in the fact of the superior age and experience of the individual so situated, so that next to the parents the eldest brother or sister is to be obeyed by the minor children of the household. And it may be considered a wise rule that the advice and direction of the eldest member of a family present at any time should be followed by the younger ones. There seems to be a natural propriety in the rule, and only extraordinary circumstances should reverse its operations.

The spiritual signification of this passage is very plainly alluded to by St. Paul [see Heb. xii., 16, 17] while exhorting the Hebrews to peace with all, lest through the excitements of contentions about worldly matters they come short of that holiness which is necessary to see the Lord—apprehend those spiritual truths which are only known by the pure in heart.

Christians' birthrights, to which they are entitled by being "born of water and the Spirit," are an inheritance in heaven–a mansion which "God has prepared for them that love Him;" joys "unspeakable and full of glory;" "a crown of glory that fadeth not away;" "eternal life," wherein they become "kings and priests unto God."

But all these privileges those who profess and call themselves Christians put in jeopardy, if they allow the follies, pleasures or riches of this earthly state to hinder them from doing their religious duties to God and their fellowmen. And how blind must they be to their own best interests who, for the sake of a few fleeting and unsatisfactory pleasures, neglect to secure a title to the Christian's privileges, and so avoid the doom of "them that know not God and that obey not the gospel of our Lord Jesus Christ." [II Thes. i., 8.]

The nineteenth chapter of Matthew, 16th—30th verses, gives a case of a young man who chose the riches of this world instead of laying up treasures in heaven, together with the instructions which our Lord gave to his disciples on the occasion.

ARTICLE X.

Rebecca and Jacob.—Gen. xxvii.

ABOUT 45 years after the events referred to in the 25th chapter, an occasion is found in which the two sons of Isaac are again brought to the notice of the readers of the book of Genesis.

Isaac had arrived at an age when he felt that he must make preparations for closing his life-work; and as a suitable manner of marking the event, he requested Esau to prepare him a feast, in the enjoyment of which he supposed he would be in a state of mind to pronounce a blessing upon him, which he expected the Lord would confirm in the future events of the life of his eldest son.

Rebecca, hearing of her husband's directions, and fearing that the result of them would bring harm to her favorite son, and frustrate the plan which the Lord had foretold in regard to the destiny of her younger son, resolves to interfere, losing sight of the fact that God is able to bring His own purposes into effect without the help of His creatures in any acts of immorality or disobedience to the rules He has given them for their conduct toward each other.

Jacob appears to have been quite passive in the matter; and although old enough to understand that lying and deception were displeasing to God, and also of an age at which he would not have been regarded as wanting in a proper respect to his mother had he declined to comply with her advice, he interposed no objections on account of the immorality of the proposed course of action, though he foresaw difficulties in carrying out the scheme, which he feared would result in bringing a curse instead of a blessing. Rebecca declared herself willing to bear the blame, and proceeded to act upon her son's hint, so as to still further deceive her husband, by putting pieces of the skins of kids upon his hands and neck, and thus cover up those sources of indentification which Jacob was shrewd enough to fear, the result of which showed his sagacity and forethought.

After making all the preparations which the mother and son could devise for effecting their object, Jacob went to his father and offered the food that Rebecca had prepared, and when questioned as to who he was, told two deliberate lies—first saying that he was Esau, and second that he had done as Isaac had bidden him. And when further questioned as to how he had found it so soon, told the third lie by declaring that the Lord had brought it to him, which was a very irreverent and seemingly unnecessary reference to the Diety, though it may, in Jacob's confusion at the unexpected question, have appeared to him as necessary in order to stop further questions, to make a reference to the divine being; or, perhaps, it was a custom in Isaac's family, to acknowledge the hand of God in the common events of life, and so from the force of habit Jacob made the assertion without serious thought, in which case the flagrancy of the sin may have been mitigated though not excused. But the father was not satisfied with his son's words, even though they were accompanied by a reference to the Diety, so he required him to come near that he might feel him and apply to him a further test of his identity, which when he had tried, confessed the belief that the story was true. Though evidently not fully satisfied in his own mind, yet he decides to proceed with the ceremonies of the occasion, and partakes of the feast which had been provided. After his appetite had been satisfied, and before pronouncing the patriarchial blessing, Isaac required his son to come near and kiss him, in which act he applied the further test of smelling, and then seems to have been fully convinced that Jacob was his first-born, and thereupon proceeded to express his wishes in regard to the future of Esau's life in which he recognized all blessings as coming from God. Though he had great wealth, he does not appear to have thought of that, or in any way to have signified his wishes as to how he would have it disposed of on that occasion.

We notice that the high state of exalted feeling which elated the father's heart, soon passed away when Esau came, in fulfillment of his father's request, and offered him the feast that he had prepared. Isaac was greatly surprised and excited at this discovery; and though apparently much displeased at the deception practiced upon him, yet he firmly decided to let the blessing remain as he had declared, confirming upon Jacob the pre-eminence which he had pronounced, when he supposed that he was his eldest son, which may possibly have been caused by his calling to mind the old story of his wife in regard to the prophecy of the younger son's superiority, and as Jacob had obtained the chief blessing, he seemed to regard the outcome of the events (so different from what he had designed,) as an indication of the Lord's will, and was disposed not only to acquiesce, but to give his sanction to a departure from the usual rule of primogeniture, in accordance with the divine decree. This decision of his father much grieved Esau, who finally obtained an inferior blessing, which under the circumstances he ought to have been satisfied with, as he had previously sold his birthright to his brother, and therefore had no rightful claim to it. But not so did the impious man regard this former oath, as he with singular obduracy and hard-heartedness, resolved that after his father's death he would slay his brother.

It now remains to notice the effect of these transactions on the after life of those who thus deceived a husband and a father. Rebecca, who first instigated the scheme, and for the love of her favorite son was willing to bear the blame, soon had her fears greatly excited on learning of Esau's design to kill his brother after her husband's death; and in order to avert such an event was constrained by her anxiety to advise Jacob to go away for a time; and, as the future events proved, she was never to see him again, though how long she lived after that, the sacred record does not inform us. She by her over-anxiety and efforts to secure the highest blessings for her favorite, wrought a feeling of deadly enmity in the mind of Esau, which probably worried her all the remaining days of her life.

And as to Jacob, the same fears exiled him from his father's house, to sojourn in a distant country, and though heir to great riches, was forced to be a hired laborer, and in that position to experience many disappointments, and during the twenty years of his absence from his home, to be continually subject to anxiety and labor both by day and by night, in summer and in winter, till at last by his industry and shrewdness he had acquired a competence; and when at last he set out for his paternal home, he was beset by grave fears for his own safety and that of his family, from the apprehended ill-will of his brother. And when that had passed, we may imagine that he must have had continual causes for irritation in the conflicting wishes of his wives, and the children of his several wives, a few of which are related; but the daily and hourly recurrence of occasions when his interference was called for to stop a quarrel or punish an offence, together with the anxiety that must have exercised his mind as the responsibility of seeing that justice was done to all, was forced upon him; so that we do not wonder that, when in his latter years, the king of Egypt inquired his age, in his reply he affirms that: "few and evil have the days of the years of my life been."

These discomforts which beset the lives of Rebecca and Jacob, and which can be fairly considered as having resulted from the deceptions practiced upon Isaac, (the sins of lying and the irreverent use of the name of the Lord) afford a lesson to Israelite and Christian people, which should deter them from ever thinking that they can please God by "doing evil" and expecting "that good may come." [Rom. iii, 8]. And therefore I earnestly exhort the readers to be always anxious to do right, leaving the Lord to work out His designs in His own way, only being careful to do their duties in that state of life in which it has pleased God to call them.

Two other cases I will refer to, which will illustrate the way in which God saw fit to deal with those who lied and endeavored to gain credence by connecting the name of the Lord with their assertions. The first is in I. Kings xiii; the second may be found in II. Chronicles, xviii. These cases were of a more aggravated character than that of Jacob, therefore they received more severe punishments.

Will not those who are addicted to the habit of profaning the name of their Creator by using it to attain wicked ends, or use it as a thoughtless prayer for curses on persons or things that happen to displease them, be warned by these cases, that He who has declared that those who take His name in vain will not be held guiltless—that they, who in this way use it worse than in vain, by seeking to advance sinful courses, by a forbidden calling on name of the Lord, will, unless they repent and amend their habits of thought and speaking, be held as guilty in His sight.

Finally, all who call themselves Christians and all who desire the blessings promised to sincere followers of Jesus Christ, I desire to remind of the words of St. Paul to the Colossians [iii, 9]: "Lie not to one another," lest you, with the father of lies, are condemned to share the fate of the devil and his angels. And also of the language of the same apostle to the Ephesians, [Eph. iv, 25,] "Wherefore, putting away lying, speak every man truth with his neighbor; for we are members one of another."

ARTICLE XI.

SHECHEM, DINAH, SIMEON AND LEVI.—Gen. xxxiv.

TWENTY-EIGHT years after the events referred to in the preceding article, some surprising events occurred in the city of Shalem, which occasioned great uneasiness and fear in Jacob's family. He had then a large number of sons, and only one daughter, who was a damsel of remarkable beauty and grace—as were her grandmother, Rebecca, and her great-grandmother Sarai,—so that she, as they did, inspired in the heart of a man in the highest rank in the country—probably the heir to the throne, an ardent desire for her as a wife.

Dinah being an only daughter was probably, allowed to do pretty much as she pleased, and choose her own associates; and her father had so many boys to look after, she very likely was left mostly to her mother's care, who, not being the best beloved of her husband, may not have been as careful, as we may suppose Rachel would, to follow Jacob's ideas in regard to her early training; and we have evidence that his religious and moral principles were less strict than those of his father and grandfather—even as it is at this period of the world's history, when people generally imagine that their fathers and grandfathers were unreasonably strict in their requirements of their children. But there is reason for fearing that, by the gradual lowering of the standard of public virtue, by the succeeding generations of our nation, it will eventually become so far below that which the Lord can consistently regard with favor, that we cannot but expect that a curse will be visited upon our people for their disregard of His laws to Whom our highest love and gratitude are due, " for our being, our reason and all the blessings of this life," and for the gracious promises of everlasting joy to those who use this life aright.

But to return to the case of Dinah. It is recorded that she "went out to see the daughters of the land." This was the carrying out of a very natural desire on the part of the young girl, who was, probably, not less than 15 and may have been 17 years old. Profane history intimates that the occasion of her going was a festival among the Shechemites—possibly the celebration of some event in their history. The new sights and sounds which greeted her eyes and ears, as she mixed with the young people and joined in their sports, must have occasioned a hilarity of feeling well calculated to bewilder her mind and lead her to readily acquiesce in any amusements which may have been proposed to her, with little or no thought of what they might lead to, and the zest with which she may have entered into the enjoyments of the occasion may have so heightened her natural beauty, that she was doubly attractive to all observers. She seemed at once to have awakened in the heart of the young prince that feeling which in these times is styled "love at first sight"; and he was so zealous in his attentions, so urgent in the manifestation of his passion, and, we may suppose, so profuse in his promises, that she allowed him to "lay with her" and defile her; though he evidently had a sincere intention of atoning for his fault by making her his wife.

What may have been the customs among the Shechemites in regard to the associations between the sexes I do not know, though I infer that they were more lax than those of the family of Jacob; but the young man being a prince, was probably in the habit of doing very much as he pleased among his young associates. He did not, as some moderns have done, after having gratified his passion, despise and leave her, but loved her and spake kindly to her; he without delay desired his father to intercede for him with Jacob to give her to him for a wife, which Hamor proceeded to do, and at the same time proposed a treaty of amity and reciprocity and offered also to Jacob and his sons the rights of citizens.

When Jacob heard of the affair, he seemed so much at a loss what to do, that he would take no action till his sons came from the field. When they arrived a consultation was held and terms agreed upon, which the Shechemites were finally prevailed upon by their rulers to consent to—by submitting to that rite which God had appointed to Abraham as the seal of his true worshipers.

Jacob's sons when they had learned of the conduct of the young prince with their sister, were grieved and very wrathful; and, notwithstanding Shechem's offer to do all he could to remedy the folly he had committed, and the agreement of the Shechemites to the terms which they had proposed as conditions for Dinah becoming the wife of the Shechemite prince, they plotted a terrible revenge, not only against the offending person, but against all the men of the city. They, as many young men in modern times have done, thought they could not do too much to punish the indignity put upon their families by the disgraceful actions of others. Two of the damsel's full brothers, Simeon and Levi, seem to have been the leaders of the plot, though the others appear to have readily acquiesced in it. The men of the city had been circumcised according to the custom of the children of Israel, and when from the effects of the operation they were incapacitated to defend themselves, these brothers, probably assisted by their servants and shepherds and herdmen, slew all the men of the city; and all this without the knowledge of their father, to whose experience, and interest in his only daughter qualified him to be the director of what was proper to be done on such an occasion. Truly, these men must have been fearfully intoxicated with the lust of revenge to have so outraged all the ideas of moral and religious equity. By their intemperate action they prevented what might have been an important missionary movement for extending the knowledge and worship of the true God; and also, they so endangered their own prospects of a peaceful residence in that region, that Jacob was directed to remove to another place.

What the immediate effects on Simeon and Levi were we are not told, though Jacob complained to them: "Ye have troubled me to make me stink among the inhabitants of the land," and he seemed to be in great fear that the subjects of King Hamor would take vengeance upon him and his sons for their slaughter of the king and nobles of the royal city, and for the sacking and spoiling of its houses and the taking captive of its women and children. And this was not a transient feeling which soon faded away, but probably embittered his whole life afterward, as may be inferred from his language on these two sons, on the occasion of his speaking his dying words to his children, when he said: "Simeon and Levi *are* brethren; instruments of cruelty *are in* their habitatations. O, my soul come not thou into their secret; unto their assembly mine honor be not thou united! for in their anger they slew a man, and in their self-will they digged down a wall. Cursed *be* their anger for *it was* fierce; and their wrath for it was cruel. I will divide them in Jacob and scatter them in Israel." [Gen. xlix, 5—7.]

I will next refer to the result to Shechem of his assault on the purity of the young girl, which his impetuous passion induced him to make. By arousing the vengeance of Dinah's brothers his life was cut short, and he was unable to fullfil his good intentions to the one who had inspired him with feelings that, when tempered by moral and religious restraints, are the most delightful that can exist between individuals of the human race ; and not only this, he was prevented from the exercise of the kingly office, in which he might have greatly benefitted his subjects and gained for himself honorable renown.

As to what was the effect on the after life of Dinah we are left to conjecture. Her brothers took her away from the young prince's house, probably against her will; and it would not be unreasonable to suppose that, after the delightful experiences of her intercourse with the young maidens of the neighborhood, and the assidious attentions of Shechem, followed as they were by the terrible tragedies which her brothers enacted, had such an effect upon her mental faculties as to render her both unfit and indisposed to assume the duties and responsibilities of a wife; and then, again, it might have been that such a stain was fixed upon her character, that no man of a sufficiently high standing socially and religiously to secure the assent of her father, ever wanted her—for it will be remembered that, at that period daughters were much more under the control of their parents, than they are at this time in our country. Her name is but once mentioned afterward in scripture history, and then only as being one of Jacob's family when he went down into Egypt, about twenty-six years later. [See chapter xlvi, 15.]

In making use of these events for the instruction of the reader, I will suggest the following cautions: Let young men who are tempted to take advantage of trusting girls and run the risk of ruining their reputations, consider that by following the bent of their inclinations, they will not only commit great sins against God and their own souls, but do an irreparable wrong to those whom they ought to respect and protect. Let young girls be assured that a man who attempts to entice them from the path of virtue, is one whose promises are of little value, and his pretended friendship is likely to prove a curse to them. And to all who are disposed to render evil to others for any real or fancied injuries, I call to their minds that the Lord hath said: "To Me *belongeth* vengeance, and recompense." [Deut. xxxii, 35; Heb. x, 30; Rom. xii, 19.]

Another affair of a similar character is related as occuring in the family of King David; see II. Sam. xiii, the final result of which is given in chapter xviii, 14—18.

ARTICLE XII.

JOSEPH'S BRETHREN.—Gen. xxxvii; xlii, 6—28.

I come now to remark upon another event which seriously affected the happiness of Jacob through the conduct of his sons.

After a long delay, his best beloved wife had borne him a son, and Rachel's son became very dear to the old man's heart. No doubt his mother took great care of him, and we have good reason for thinking that she was judicious in the management of the lad, because he seemed to be an extraordinary good boy.

The older sons of Jacob continued to conduct themselves wickedly when their father was not with them, so much so, that Joseph could not forbear telling Jacob of their evil doings, which probably was the cause of their receiving reproofs, and also was a reason for a dislike for the conscientious boy; for wicked persons are sure to hate those who report their misdeeds.

But their father's partiality appears to have been manifested in an unwise way, by providing him with an extra gay coat, which seems to have set his young mind to dreaming—which dreams seemed to portend his future pre-eminence over his brethren, and with great simplicity he told them to the family, thereby increasing the hatred which the brothers had cherished toward him; and even the father reproved him for what he appeared to think was an unwise mention of his youthful fancies; and yet the impression which the relation made upon the old man's mind was such, that he gave particular attention to his favorite boy, with a seeming feeling of expectation that the dreams were a prophetic intimation of events in the future, as the subsequent history of the children of Israel proved them to be.

In this connection I will make the remark that, perhaps God does still visit his servants in visions of the night, for their comfort or warning; and that there is wisdom in reflecting upon what seems to come to our minds when the body is sleeping. The writer cannot testify from his own experience of benefit derived from his own dreaming, but he does know of a case where a friend was relieved of anxiety on his account, by a dream which revealed to her circumstances of which she was not aware, but which proved to be true.

But notwithstanding the ill-will which his brothers exhibited to Joseph, he seems to have cherished a proper feeling toward his father's sons, as well as a filial and obedient spirit to his father, being ready to undertake a somewhat hazardous journey to satisfy his father's anxiety as to their welfare. After arriving at the place to which he had been sent, and not finding his brethren, instead of giving up the undertaking, he went in search of them—extending his travels some ten or fifteen miles in order to find them, so that he could tell his father of their welfare and the condition of the flocks and herds.

When Joseph came in sight of his brethren, they showed the bitter enmity they had towards him by conspiring to take his life, with the declared intention of bringing the indications of his dreams to nought, and they were only prevented from carrying out their plan by the non-concurrence of Reuben; but with a cruelty to their father scarcely less than would have been the killing of their brother, they contrived a scheme to deceive him into the belief that Joseph had been devoured by wild beasts, which so grieved the bereaved father that he refused to be comforted by all the efforts which his children could make to alleviate his sorrow, for he declared: "I will go down into the grave, unto my son, mourning."

Thus was the famous patriarch, (whose name had been changed by the Lord to "Israel," which name has been perpetuated in the history of the most wonderful nation of the world,) rendered miserable and unhappy during his declining years, through the wickedness of his children, occasioned by his own fault in permitting his family to live in disobedience to the rules of godliness. It is true he had great difficulties to encounter in the conflicting wishes of his four wives, and the stubborn and reckless behavior of his many children, which would very likely have been avoided, had he been permitted to have his beloved Rachel only, with whom he could have lived in peace and sympathy, and trained up their children to be, as was his son Joseph, a benefactor of his time, and a model of a wise statesman and a faithful public servant.

It may be observed that both Abraham and Jacob, of their own choice, were contented with a single wife, if they had been permitted to have the one of their choice, though they both took other wives—the first, because he was solicited to do so by his beloved Sarah, as a means of remedying her own inability, that her husband might have an heir; but when at last her own defects had been removed, and she became a mother indeed, trouble sprang up in the family, which led to bad results; and the second, because the father of the girl of his choice deceived him by giving him the wrong daughter, and so he was constrained by his ardent affection for Rachel, to take a second wife; and when she was incapable of bearing children, she importuned her husband to take her handmaid as a wife, so that she could adopt her servant's children as her own; and as Leah also claimed, and obtained the same privilege in behalf of her handmaid, Jacob found himself encompassed with a quadrupled amount of responsibility, which must have filled his mind with constant anxiety, amidst the active rivalry of the contending interests of the four women who claimed his affection and protection. No wonder that the harmony and morals of the family suffered in the contests.

It is not the purpose of this article to pursue the future history of Joseph in detail, but so much of it is pertinent, as will prove the true prophetic character of his dreams. Though sold as a slave, he, by his faithfulness to every trust confided to him, won the unbounded confidence of his master, and though falsely charged and imprisoned, he maintained a high degree of integrity, and a firm trust in God; and by God's providential ordering he was raised to the responsible position of governor of Egypt, in which position he received the prophesied acts of homage by his brethren.

It may be of interest to remark, that the children of Israel received 20 pieces of silver for the first slave they sold to foreign slave-traders; but they had to undergo hundreds of years of servitude themselves, and loss of hundreds of thousands of men in the wilderness, before they got the bones of Joseph back to the land of Canaan. These judgments, we may suppose, were visited upon them, for their own wickedness, in connection with the wickedness of the original Canaanites, among whom they dwelt.

Another case of similar character, where a brother plotted against a brother, occurred in the case when Absalom conspired and murdered Ammon, though Ammon was really a guilty man and deserved punishment; an account of which may be found in the second book of Samuel xiii, 23—37.

St. Paul to the Romans, [chap. xii, 10,] exhorts Christians to "Be kindly affectioned one to another with brotherly love," with such an affection as is suitable to the relation of persons having the same parents, and whose welfare and honor are very closely bound together, as they, in a more important sense, are related to each other—being the adopted children of God, through Christ, and heirs of an everlasting inheritance together; so we should cherish a sincere and unselfish regard for each other.

But mankind is so "very far gone from original righteousness," that instances are not infrequent where persons holding this relationship to each other, have become irreconcilable enemies; so that Solomon's experience led him to make a proverb to the effect that, "A brother offended *is harder to be won* than a strong city; and their contentions *are* like the bars of a castle." [Prov. xviii, 19.] Therefore, it is imperative that all who desire to obtain a disposition of heart in accord with God's requirements, that they give all diligence to become such characters as He can permit to share the felicities "which God hath prepared for them that love Him." [I. Cor., ii, 9.]

ARTICLE XIII.

HEROD THE GREAT.—Matt. ii; 1—18.

HAVING made remarks upon the recorded actions of quite a number of individuals mentioned in the Old Testament history, with the view of showing how God dealt with them for the short-comings in their duties to Him and their fellow-men, and the effects of such acts upon others, in the previous twelve articles, I now turn to the New Testament with the design of considering in the same general way, a few of the cases there related—either historical events or parabolic illustrations by our Lord,—with the same object in view, that of warning the readers against yielding to the temptations of the world, the flesh and the devils; as they will, if not resisted and repented of, lead them into forgetfulness of God, if not into open rebellion against Him, and result in "everlasting destruction from the presence of the Lord," [II Thes. i, 9.]—who will take "vengeance on them that know not God, and that obey not the gospel of our Lord Jesus Christ," [verse 8.]

The first case presented is that related in the second chapter of Matthew, where it is recorded that learned men arrived at the city of Jerusalem, making inquiries for a prophesied Prince of the Jewish nation, declaring that while in their own country they had seen His Star; and they were so impressed with its strange appearance that they thought it wise to make a long journey to bespeak his favor, by rendering their homage to one who was so wonderfully heralded by the movements of the heavenly bodies.

A great commotion occurred in Jerusalem when

HEROD AND THE WISE MEN.

HEROD AND THE PRIESTS.

these men appeared and made known their errand. The so-called king (though he was only a governor, appointed by a Roman Emperor,) because he supposed that in case a real king of the Jews, who was appointed by God through authenticated prophesies should come to the throne of David, he would take from his family the authority and privileges they were enjoying; the Herodian party, because if the reigning dynasty were overthrown, their present honors and emoluments would be lost; and the priests and people, because they knew that, before the power of the Romans could be overthrown great battles would have to be fought, and long and arduous struggles with the greatest military power on earth would be necessary, and they, although they felt greatly annoyed by the subjugated condition in which they were held, had not the patriotism and bravery necessary to urge them on to a struggle to obtain what they desired. But there were a few, like the shepherds, who on receiving the announcement of his birth from the angelic host, hastened to Bethlehem, and when they had seen Him, reported abroad the story told them by the angel, [Luke ii, 8—20]; or like Simon and Anna, who greeted the young prince with satisfied desire and joyful hope, and having a more definite comprehension of the character of Christ's kingdom, gave their testimony to the great things that might be expected from Him.

Herod, in order to learn the exact facts in regard to the prophecies concerning the Christ, applied to the authorized teachers of the scriptures, the chief priests, together with the scribes, whose business was to copy the sacred writings, (a business akin to the printing of bibles in these days,) for the information which the learned strangers asked for, and when it was obtained, he sent them to Bethlehem, enjoining upon them to let him know if they found the young child, pretending that he desired to pay the Heaven-appointed King the worship due to Him.

The travelers from the east went to Bethlehem, and guided by the star, readily discovered the young child, though in circumstances quite different from what they probably expected, for, instead of a palace and surrounded by circumstances of worldly grandeur which usually attend the princes of the world, they found only apparently a couple of poor peasants, lodged in a humble dwelling, with their child, not clothed in garments prepared for Him, but wrapped in cloths swathed about His body, indicating that the parents were unable to supply their child with the most ordinary garments. But, notwithstanding these adverse appearances, these men of science and learning seem not to have wavered in their faith, that the infant before them was the person who had been prophesied of, and the one for whom the star had been sent to guide them to His presence; and so they presented their homage both by acts and gifts, no doubt well satisfied that they had attained the object of their journey; but having had dreams which they interpreted as warnings that it was God's will that they should not return to Herod, they went back to the east by another route.

To return to the case of Herod, whose conduct in this affair contains the warning which this article is designed to enforce, when he found that the wise men did not heed his desire to be informed of the discovery of the child, was very wroth, and showed the duplicity which he tried to practice on the eastern visitors, by ordering that the children two years old and under, that were in Bethlehem and the coasts thereof, should be slain, thinking that in that way he could thwart God's purposes. The cruel order was executed, but failed of its object, for God warned Joseph by a dream to flee into Egypt, and so he was saved from the slaughter which was visited on those little ones, whom Christians in all ages since that time have styled "holy innocents," and thus they have received honors and remembrances which have been given to no other equal number of infants since the world began. But for that act Herod's name stands out in bold relief in the world's history as one of the most heartless and cruel of the human race, and his name is likely to be held in detestation as long as the world endures, by all who cherish the ordinary feelings of humanity, and especially by those who have learned its highest and holiest emotions and manifestations, as embodied in the teachings of the God-man, and exhibited in the lives of many of His disciples in all ages since His earthly life was finished.

Herod was intoxicated with the extravagant ideas that he must, at every risk, secure the government to his family, and that he had the power to change the purposes of God, which had been declared by prophet after prophet, whose teachings had been accepted by the Jewish nation as the Lord's revealed will, and further attested by the extraordinary journey and wonderful story of the most learned and scientific men of that age of the world. But though Herod may have had some idea that his cruel scheme succeeded in putting an end to the probability of a rival to his family in the government of Judea, his life did not long survive these events. We may be sure that any time he may have had for calm reflections on the results of this act, could not have afforded him any satisfaction—unless his soul had become so imbued with a devilish spirit that he could delight in sorrow, wickedness and blood.

To apply the warning of this subject to the people of this age and country: Those who reject the christian system now, are as strangely blinded by their passions and prejudices, as was Herod the tetrarch, when, in spite of the testimony of God verified by the most wonderful miraculous manifestations—in spite of the testimony of the wisest and purest of men in every age of the world, they neglect to accept the offers of eternal life and joy, made in the gospel of the Son of God by the King of Kings and Lord of Lords, choosing instead the fleeting but unsatisfactory pleasures of this world, which will soon end with each one of them—they know not how soon. They seem willing to live lives of disobedience to God's laws, cherishing thoughts and passions at variance with His will, and even at variance with what their own consciences must assure them is right and true; with no well-founded hope of happiness when this life is ended; "but a certain fearful looking for of judgment and fiery indignation which shall devour the adversaries" of God. [Heb. x, 27.]

Another similar instance is recorded in I Sam. [xviii—xxiv chapters,] where Saul sought to destroy David, whom God had selected to be his successor.

God commanded the children of Israel, "Thou shalt not kill," [Ex. xx, 13,] and Christ explains the spirit of the commandment by saying, "Whosoever is angry with his brother without a cause" violates it; [Matt. vi, 22,] and John in explaining it to the seven churches in Asia, wrote: "Whosoever hateth his brother is a murderer." [I John iii, 15.]

ARTICLE XIV.

HEROD ANTIPAS, HERODIAS.—Mark vi, 14—29.

THE next event which is given in the gospels, that affords a suitable subject for this series of articles, happened about thirty years after the event related in the second chapter of Matthew. The principal character in the narrative was a son of "Herod the Great," who had obtained the government over a portion of the territory over which his father reigned. His character seems to have been less cruel and impetuous than his father's, and so he was more open to the intrigues and designs of others. Indeed, had he not been thus influenced, it is likely that he would have become a disciple both of John the Baptist and of Jesus.

During Herod's administration of the government, a wonderful preacher appeared in the country, whose startling predictions of a great event about to occur, and indignant denunciations of the wickedness which prevailed among people of all degrees, and earnest exhortations to repentance, were delivered with a power, directness and pathos which awakened the attention of the people of a wide section of the country, who attended upon his preaching, many of whom were convinced of their sins, promised repentance, and received a baptism as a testimony of their belief of the predictions, doctrines and duties that were the burden of his discourses.

Among the interested hearers of the great preacher was Herod, who heard him gladly and did many things to which he had been exhorted by John. But he did not bring forth fruit meet for repentance, by forsaking all that he knew to be sins against God—for he had taken as a wife, not only the wife of another man, but a woman whose relation to him was such that it was impossible for her to become his wife without violating God's law given through Moses. John had plainly rebuked him for this sin, but without inducing him to repent of it—he still kept on in the course of disobedience; though he did not seem to be very seriously offended with the prophet for his plain preaching.

But not so did Herodias, his partner in this sin, regard the messenger of the Lord; for she set about contriving a scheme for accomplishing his death. She was not able to succeed by any direct influence upon Herod, but by taking the occasion of his birth-day festival, when he had invited his lords, high captains and the wealthiest of his subjects to a supper, and when they had feasted upon the choicest viands of the country, and partaken freely of the richest wines of the vintage, and had become oblivious to serious business, she sent her beautiful daughter, arrayed, no doubt, in brilliant apparel, to dance before the company, which so pleased Herod that, in his inebriated condition, he promised with an oath that he would give her whatever she would ask, even to the half of his kingdom. The damsel went to her mother for advice as to what she should ask, who perceiving that it was a favorable opportunity to wreak her vengeance upon the faithful preacher, immediately instructed her daughter to ask the head of John the Baptist; and the daughter seemed ready to obey her mother, and she made the demand forthwith.

Never, perhaps, was a person more astonished at any unexpected choice of a woman, than was Herod at the unmaidenly request of the radiant girl, for while he would have willingly satisfied to the utmost the ordinary desires of the female heart, he was very sorry that she had asked such a murderous act as a favor; but because he had promised with an oath in the presence of such a company, he felt constrained to keep his promise, which he did by ordering an executioner to behead the man whom Jesus declared to be the greatest prophet who had ever been born, and whom he, himself, regarded as just and holy.

We may readily conceive how this heinous act must have disquieted Herod's conscience, as soon as the excitement of the occasion and the intoxication caused by the beverages had produced, passed away; one illustration of which is shown by the fact that, when the report of the miracles which Jesus did came to him, his conclusion was that He was John the Baptist who was risen from the dead.

If this was the only unjust act (though probably it was not,) of Herod's administration, the Emperor of Rome had good reason for taking from him his office and banishing him to Lyons, a city of Gaul, whither Herodias accompanied him. They must have ended their lives in a condition of disappointment and unhappiness which only christian virtue and hope would have enabled them to bear cheerfully; but that condition of mind, it is probable, they never attained.

It is indispensable to a genuine repentance, that it should include everything known to be displeasing to God—the hearing the preached word, and doing only a part of the duties commanded will never result in a full salvation.

In our own days the preachers of the gospel are often reviled, their warnings made light of, and their proffered assistance scorned by those who most need their help; so much is this the case that, no doubt, many of Christ's ambassadors are greatly discouraged in their efforts to awaken their hearers to a proper sense of the dangers that threaten those who, year after year delay the commencement of the work of preparing their hearts for the pleasures which are at God's right hand, till so late a period, that there is little probability that they will ever be able to acquire that relish for holy truths and holy employments, without which the society of the Lord, the holy angels and the spirits of the just made perfect will be uncongenial company. If we do not learn to delight in these things during our earthly days of probation, we may reasonably expect that we should never be able to enjoy them, even were we to be admitted to the locality of the blessed of God.

The only other spiritual condition made known in God's word is a state of hostility to all that is good and and holy, in company with the devil and his angels, and with those of earth who rejected the offers of the Christ's salvation and ceased not to work wickedness; from which condition there will be no hope of relief.

Similar cases are those of Ahab and Jezebel. Corresponding events in their history are related in I. Kings xviii, 13; xxi, 5—16; II. Kings ix, 30--37.

ARTICLE XV.

THE UNTHANKFUL SUBJECTS.—Matt. xxii; 2—14.

ALTHOUGH the parables of our Lord may not have the pertinency in the minds of some people, as the actual facts of history, with which to illustrate the folly of sin, and the danger of being lead into wickedness by our own selfish desires, yet in them, we may believe, that there are illustrations of God's dealings with men, which we are less liable to mistake the exact lesson intended to be taught, than when we make our own conclusions upon the facts which have come to our knowledge of the past.

It is supposed that most of Jesus' parables are founded on actual events—being, as it were, a sort of paraphrases—and that they may be considered in their earthly parts, as having actually happened, to which Jesus made instructive applications, by showing how they portray the principles upon which God acts in His dealings with mankind.

The parable that we find related by St. Matthew, which I have chosen to consider, is entitled the marriage feast of the King's son, in which God the Father is represented as having given out invitations to the wedding, and at the proper time, as sending his servants to call them that were bidden, (the children of Israel,) to the marriage, (Christ being the bridegroom, and the Church the bride); but those who had received the messages neglected the call. Passing over the first slight, the King again sent his servants with a more urgent message and giving additional reasons why there

THE UNTHANKFUL SUBJECTS.

should be no further delay in attending to the summons; but the second messages are again treated with disdain and the messengers met with insults by the principal ones, who went to their usual avocations, as though the King's wishes and the interests of the kingdom were of no consequence to them, while the less civilized people treated them with insults, cruelty and death, indicating the persecutions which the early disciples received.

At this the King was angry, and sent his soldiers who destroyed those murderers and burned their city, (which prefigured the destruction of Jerusalem under Titus.)

But that the festal preparations shall not have been made in vain, the King directed the servants to go out into the highways and bring in all that they found, both bad and good, declaring that those who had been invited were not worthy.

I will now briefly state the meaning of the parable as understood by learned commentators: the Kingdom of Heaven represents the laws of the Christian Dispensation as administered by the authority of the Lord Jesus, the Christ of the Prophets, and the King of the Saints; the King represents God the Father Almighty; the Son represents Jesus; though nothing is said of a bride, other scriptures represent the Christian Church as the bride.—[See Eph. v, 25—27, 32; and Rev. xix, 7, 9.]; the servants were John the Baptist, and the first preachers of the gospel, those invited were the children of Israel, who were invited long before by Moses and other prophets, and this call was to remind them that the feast was ready; the feast will be the blessings and joys of a true christian life and the rest of the Heavenly state after the resurrection; the other servants, the later preachers of the gospel in apostolic

THE UNTHANKFUL SUBJECTS. 81

times; the armies of the King, the Roman armies; their city, Jerusalem; the inviting people from the highways, represent the calling of the gentiles.

Marriages are occasions, when so much happiness is anticipated by the bridegroom and bride, that they usually desire that all their friends should so far sympathize with them as to wish them well, not only by inward feelings, but by outward manifestations; and the same is probably true of most of the young friends of the young couple, who doubtless feel that the cheering circumstances by which they are surrounded, may be hoped for themselves also, in the near future.

It should be noted however that marriage feasts, at the time that Jesus spake this parable, at least among the higher classes, (and the parable represents a marriage of the very highest class) were continued for several days.

The parable is designed to represent a heavenly state of things, which can only be faintly paralleled by the arrangements of earthly society. One particular in which earthly feasts fail to fully represent the heavenly feast is the character and attributes of the maker of the feast—the Great Jehovah, the Creator and sustainer of all things, the omnipotent, omnipresent and omniscient being, who has no equal among created beings, though His only-begotten Son claimed, and was acknowledged to be His equal in dignity by the greatest and most versatile writer of the New Testament. Witness the following verses:

"Who being the brightness of *His* [God's] glory and the express image of His person, and upholding all things by the word of His power, when He had by Himself purged our sins, sat down at the right hand of the Majesty on high; . . . . . . Unto the Son *He*

82 THE UNTHANKFUL SUBJECTS.

saith, Thy throne, O God *is* forever and ever; a sceptre of righteousness *is* the sceptre of thy kingdom," [Heb. i, 3, 8.]

The Israelites had been notified before of this feast by Moses and the other prophets, who had prophesied of the Messiah, and the blessings which He would give to those who should believe the good tidings and obey the gospel. [See Deut. xviii, 15, 18; Jer. xxiii, 5; Is. vii, 14; xi, 1—5; lxii, 11; xxv, 6, 9; Micah. v, 2.] The announcement that the feast was ready was made by John the Baptist, [See Matt. iii, 11, 12]; by God the Father, [See Matt. iii, 17]; by Jesus himself, [Matt. iv, 17; v, 3 to chap. vii, 28]; by his disciples. Matt. x, 5 —42 contains Jesus' instructions to them; also Luke x, 1—17; and after the day of Pentecost, the apostles and first christian preachers, [See Acts ii, 1—36; iii, 12 —26; iv, 8—12; v, 29—32; vii, 37—38; viii, 26—35; ix, 17—22; x, 34—44; xi, 22—26; xiii, 44—49.]

I will now note the character and dignity of those who were invited to the feast. They were the descendants of Abraham, through Isaac and Jacob, and heirs of the promises which God made to that patriarch, who was and is most honored of any mere man since the creation of the world; they had many times failed in their duty to God, who had punished them for their sins, and many times, on their repentance, had pardoned them for Abraham's sake; they had been favored by the Lord with special revelations of His will, which was their law, which is believed to be, so far as relates to the first principles of moral conduct superior to that given to any other nation of ancient times; and that part of it styled "the decalogue," or ten commandments, cannot be surpassed by the wisest legislators; and it is certain that if its spirit could find just exemplification in the lives of all mankind, this earth would be a happy world, and would need no other laws. This law was sometimes obeyed by the Israelites, when they were prosperous and happy, at other times they neglected the commandments of the Lord and suffered for it. When at last their Messiah came, who proved his claims by many wonderful works, and because he seemed not to answer their expectations, they as a nation rejected him, since which time, in accordance with the predictions of that Messiah, [Jesus], they have been scattered all over the civilized world; have lost their nationality, though they retain characteristics that are peculiar to the descendants of Abraham, Isaac and Jacob. God, by a special appointment, chose them to be the keepers of His written revelation to mankind, which they kept faithfully from generation to generation, till the era of the Christian Dispensation; and to descendants of Abraham we are indebted for the christian scriptures, which inform us more fully of the nature of the great marriage-feast which all who will accept the offers of the gospel are invited to partake.

Why did these people act so unwisely? The maker of the feast was of a sufficient dignity to command their respect, and His Son was equal to His Father in all qualities that call for honor and gratitude, for He had made great sacrifices for their welfare; they were the favored subjects of the King, and as such would naturally have been proud of the honor of being guests on so great an occasion. How could it have happened that they were so ready to excuse themselves from attendance at the marriage-feast in honor of the Prince, on such slight pretexts; to treat His servants with insult, or with barbarity to so great a degree as to justify the King in visiting punishments due to murderers and rebels upon them? Plainly it was, in some cases, because they felt too proud of their own inferior dignity to accept with satisfaction any favors from one of a higher degree; in others, because attendance at the feast would interfere with their own selfish plans; in others, because they rebelled against the authority of the King, and were determined to resist His claims by all the means in their power, not considering that the invitation was prompted by generosity, and that His laws were their best security for peace and prosperity among themselves. They esteemed the everlasting rest typified by the feast, as less desirable than the short season of earthly pleasures, mixed as they were, with toil and anxiety and disappointments; although they must have known that by thus manifesting their ingratitude they would displease a King from whom they received all that they had—even their being, and who delights in the welfare of the good and virtuous, though unalterably opposed to the wicked and vicious —yet willing to pardon sinners who repent them truly of their former sins, steadfastly purposing to lead a new life, have a lively faith in the King's mercy through the merits of the Prince, and be in charity with all men.

God, as the King of the Universe, uses various agencies to accomplish his purposes, both in blessing His subjects when they are faithful, and in punishing them when they are rebellious. In the case of the Jews in Christ Jesus' time, He used the Roman armies to punish them for their rejection of the gospel; they destroyed Jerusalem about forty years after this parable was spoken by the Lord.

The order to the servants to "go out into the highways and as many as ye shall find bid to the marriage," likely refers to the offer made to the Gentiles to participate in the blessings of the gospel. Before this none but the descendants of Abraham through

Isaac and Jacob were considered as entitled to a full share in the blessings promised—though the gentiles were admitted to some of the privileges on becoming proselytes, they were debarred from having a share in the administration of the government, and also were not entitled to a share in the distribution of the land in the year of Jubilee.

The servants are related to have succeeded in securing a sufficient number of guests; it then became of interest to the King to see the guests, and He came in to scrutinize them—to see if they were all right. Did they appear cheerful, and thankful, and happy, and appreciative of the good will of the King? Were there any who cherished a spirit of rebellion against the rules of the kingdom, or the authority of the Prince? If so, they were not suitable guests for such an occasion.

To make this King a proper representative of God, we must consider Him as having unlimited authority over the lives and conditions of his subjects; and when we consider this fact, we may readily perceive how very unreasonable and imprudent were those who would not forego the usual labors of a day for the sake of conciliating His favor on whom they were so deeply dependent; and still more infatuated must they have been with the affairs of their every-day life, as well as jealous of any suspected attempt to interfere with their own selfish schemes, who could requite His goodness with insult and cruelty.

There was one who evidently had taken no pains to appear in clothing suitable for the feast; perhaps he had only the garb in which he did his ordinary work; perhaps they were ragged and slovenly put on, indicating that the man was wanting in a proper regard for the proprieties of the high festival, or even that he had designed by his want of care to appear agreeable, to insult not only the King and the Prince, but the other guests also. If he had had a reasonable excuse very likely he would have given it when the King asked for one; but he had none to give. This being the case, we may easily imagine the justice of the sentence pronounced by the King:

"Bind him hand and foot, and take him away, and cast him into outer darkness, there shall be weeping and gnashing of teeth."

These phrases of the parable may signify that those persons are liable to make a serious mistake who suppose that they can secure and enjoy the blessings of the gospel, reaching beyond death and the resurrection of the body, without a sincere love for Christ, a hearty repentance of sin, and a humble trust in the merits of the Savior, [the wedding garment,] for pardon, for they will be discovered, rendered helpless, so that no efforts of their own can be of any avail to save themselves, with no hope of relief from a sorrow so intense that the whole body and mind will be nerved up to a high degree of excitement occasioned by the pangs of torment which they will suffer.

The phrase "For many are called but few chosen," plainly indicates that the man spoken of represents a large majority of those invited. In view of this truth how careful should we be in judging ourselves as to our religious condition, lest we fail to make our "calling and election sure."

Another remark may be added in relation to the care taken by the King that no one unworthy of the great occasion should be allowed to participate in the feast. It is by this care and oversight that the maker of the feast will secure a bride for His Son which will entail no disgrace upon His government. The Church, in order to be a suitable bride for her Lord, must be purified from all that is sinful—past sins repented of and pardoned, and the righteousness of the Saints, who have washed their robes and made them white in the blood of the Lamb, [Rev. vii, 14,] typified by "fine linen, clean and white," [Rev. xix, 8,] must cover her, so that her appearance shall be appropriate as a companion of one who is " glorious in holiness."

In gaining the instruction which our Lord designed that we should receive from this parable, we may consider that the enjoyments which sincere christians will experience in the reflection that they are under the special care of an all-wise and all-powerful being, who has authorized them to call Him by the endearing title of "Father,"—and as a loving child rejoices in fulfiling the desires of its parents, so they are delighted with doing whatever is made known to them as their heavenly Father's will, even as Jesus gave them the precept: "My meat is to the will of Him that sent me; [John iv, 34], and set them the example by going about doing good, both by teaching and healing; and on another occasion, He gave them a command, as a test—an outward and visible sign by which they could assure themselves that they possessed a true obedient spirit and grateful remembrance of His love for them—to make feast of bread and wine, in which act He assured them that He would be with them, as in some sense the bread and wine would be His body and blood; [1 Cor. xi, 23—26.] Another quality of this feast is, that it is satisfying, and they who partake of it with a healthy spiritual appetite want nothing better—it being easy for them "to be contented and do [their] duty in that state of life in which it hath pleased God to call [them.] " And still another quality of the gospel feast is, that it will never end—it will strengthen and refresh God's children all through this life, and when they are called to rest from their earthly labors, they close their earthly visions with the blessed hope that they will be raised and "awake . . . to everlasting life," [Dan. xii, 2,] while the same passage teaches that those who reject the invitation, or do not make suitable preparations to appear at the feast, shall awake . . . . . "to shame and everlasting contempt."

How very profound and overpowering must be the intoxication with the common employments of the world, that affects those people who are continually seeking their highest enjoyments in the "things that perish with the using," [Col. ii, 22,] and which their bodies, ere long will be disqualified for enjoying; which induces them to neglect the means for preparing their souls for the employments and enjoyments of the heavenly state, which will never cease with those who are qualified to take pleasure in them.

ARTICLE XVI.

THE FAITHFUL SERVANT, WHO MAY BECOME AN EVIL SERVANT.—Mark xiii, 34; Matt. xxiv, 45—51; Mark xiii, 35—37.

I have the opinion of a learned commentator, that the passages above referred to are best to be read in the order noted above, as in that way a complete statement is made that refers to the same subject; and also for considering it as a warning to christian ministers.

Mark xiii, 34 states that "*the Son of man* (meaning the Christ,) is as a man taking a far journey, who left his his house, and gave authority to his servants, and to every man his work, and commanded the porter to watch." Those having authority are understood to be the authorized teachers of the gospel, the porter or gate-keeper may mean one of them who had a special duty in regard to the others—a bishop perhaps.

In Matt. xxiv, 45, the question is asked: "Who then is a faithful and wise servant" who will be entrusted with authority and duties respecting the others? and in verse 26 is mentioned the privileges and honors which will be bestowed on him, if he finally be found faithful. This much in regard to the first part of the parable.

But as these articles are designed to warn the reader against the influences which tend to evil doing, I will now pass to the examination of the latter part of the parable.

In considering the 47th verse, I will suppose that the reputed "wise and faithful servant" has been successful in gaining the confidence of his Lord, and secured the appointment of overseer of all the others, and having entered upon his duties; yet there is still a peradventure in the case, therefore Jesus intimates that he may become an "evil servant" by the significant word "but," which commences the 48th verse, and proceeds to state what he (the servant) may think, after waiting a long time: "My lord delayeth his coming"—perhaps he will never come; and then carries the thought into action by severe and unwarranted behavior towards his inferiors, and takes and uses the goods entrusted to his care for his own selfish enjoyments, amounting, perhaps, to gluttony and intoxication; then, it may be, that the porter, in the midst of the disorder and revelry occuring in the household, will relax his watchfulness, so that it will be quite certain that the return of the lord will be at a time when the servants were not expecting him, and in conditions of body and mind unprepared to receive the long-absent owner of the goods that have been put to such evil uses.

Perhaps it may seem somewhat presumptuous for a layman to undertake to criticize the servants of the Lord; but on the reflection that it may be profitable to them to know how their sayings and doings appear from the laymen's stand-point, I am led to make my thoughts upon the subject public in the hope that our reverend teachers may, if they perceive that we have not learned their lessons correctly, see what our misconceptions are, and so be better qualified to give us the instructions we need. I may state further that I was, as it were, born into the ministerial fraternity, being the son of a clergyman and having another for my maternal grandfather, and still another for a great-great-grandfather; and by counting back less than a dozen generations, I have learned that some of my ancestors were near relatives of one of the archbishops of Canterbury, the pri-

THE EVIL SERVANT. 91

mate (or chief minister) of the English Church; and having been faithfully taught by my parents my duty to God and christian people, for which I cherish a grateful remembrance; and I believe that I have, by God's assistance, not entirely failed in fulfiling the hopes of my parents and christian friends, though far from claiming perfection in the christian life. Under these circumstances I hope to be believed when I assert that I have no prejudices against christian ministers.

To the ordinary Christian, who only judges by what is observed at the present time, it may seem that the clergy of these times (especially those who preach the doctrines which any particular Christian supposes to be the true ones,) might be excepted from the liability to relapse into a condition in which they will care more for the pleasures of the world than for their religious duties; yet when they examine further, and discover the various and conflicting opinions which the different classes of those who "profess and call themselves Christians have of the ministers of others than those of their own sect, most religious people will concede that some of them must be in danger from that source. And if they study the past history of the christian religion, they will find that from the first, particularly since the time that the early persecutions ceased, that the clergy have been, are now and may be expected in the future to be subject to temptations to relax their watchings and indulge their prejudices and give way to their passions, which shows that the cautions which Jesus gave to His disciples was and is needed to secure even the bound servants of the Lord from losing the reward which is set before them as the result of faithfulness in their high calling.

The first step in a relaxation of the commanded watching is doubt in relation to the promises of God, expressed by the thought, "My Lord delayeth his coming." The servant becomes impatient of the long waiting, and as "hope deferred maketh the heart sick," he seeks relief from the monotony of the long vigils by studying how he may pass the time more agreeably than by continuing to discharge the duties which have been entrusted to him. If he continues in this state of mind it will not be long before he will be found using with more and more prodigality his Master's property that had been confided to him, with little or no regard to the directions enjoined upon him, and banishing from his thoughts all ideas of his responsibility and the certainty that he will be called to account for his neglect and the result of it. It may be expected that, from cherishing these thoughts he will soon proceed to words —using his authority over the other servants and directing a new departure which will nullify the Lord's commands, and to actions, by engaging in employments contrary to all precedents established by the directions and customs of the Master, so much so that, when the Master does return, he will find every thing in the house in such a condition of disorder—so contrary to the system which He had established, that He will severely punish the wicked servant and banish him to the society of hypocrites; and thus he will fail of the great reward, the contemplation of which will occasion a degree of disappointment which is aptly expressed by "weeping and gnashing of teeth."

In the past ages, when has it not been(since the expiration of the first three hundred years of the christian era,) that some clergymen have not been ardent seekers for worldly honors, worldly wealth, worldly power and worldly pleasures?—seeming to have taken little heed to the advice of Jesus' most faithful disciple: "Love not the world neither the things *that are* in the world."

[I. John ii, 15.] Many, indeed, have given evidence by their lives, of a sincere desire to obey the directions given them in the scriptures; but there have been notable exceptions, which have shown that some of them have been more anxious to secure the applause of men than the favor of God.

At the present time there seems to be many who claim to have been called by the Lord to be his ambassadors, and whose claims are acknowledged as genuine by christian people, who appear anxious to be clothed in fine linen and fare sumptuously, instead of being careful to follow the example and teachings of Jesus: "Be not therefore anxious saying, what shall we eat or what shall we drink or wherewithal shall we be clothed." [Matt. vi, 31; Revised version.] I find no fault with moderate efforts to secure comfortable food that will promote health, and raiment so as to appear agreeable to those with whom we associate, provided it is done without owing anything to any one; but to seek after such things with the degree of anxiety that worldly men exhibit, betokens that a minister needs the warnings that his Master has given.

And has it not in these days been often the case that ministers who have acquired a commanding position among their brethren, are disposed to be overbearing and inconsiderate of the feelings and convictions of their less prominent brethren, when they do not happen to agree with those who assume to be the leaders in their society? and in so doing do they not violate the directions which the Christ gave to His apostles? [Mark x, 42—44]; and in the next verse He states the fact that his own example is a pattern for them to follow in their intercourse with each other.

But I have not the space to pursue this course of remarks further; and it seems to me unnecessary to do so, as I suppose our reverend brethren are able to add pertinent thoughts on the subject, and make applications to themselves, with greater force than their humble brother could, who takes the liberty to remind them that the great apostle to the Gentiles once expressed a fear for himself that, after preaching to others, he should be a castaway. [I. Cor. ix, 27.]

I will next state what I suppose to be some of the characteristics of a christian minister which appear to me most likely to secure the confidence of the average laymen: 1st—Humility with a determination not to think of himself more highly than he ought to think; 2d—Studious, seeking to know the truth of God, as contained in the holy scriptures, striving to teach its most important truths faithfully, and at the same time carefully abstaining from going beyond the teachings of the Christ; 3d—Prayerful, for the aid of the Holy Spirit to guide his mind to a right understanding of his duty both to God and to the people of his charge; 4th—A disposition to conduct himself impartially toward his brethren of all degrees—not despising the poor nor truckling for the favor of the rich, and anxiously endeavoring to lead the rich, the poor, the learned and the ignorant to the knowledge of and obedience to God's will as made known in the gospels; 5th—Contentment, not disposed to repine if worldly adversity is his portion, showing the poor how to endure privation with christian patience, nor unduly elated when temporal prosperity comes to him, setting an example of liberality to the wealthy; 6th—Aptness to teach, not only in the sense of being able to make plain to ordinary minds the religious truths that seem to them difficult to comprehend, but in the more common acceptation of the word "apt," a readiness to give instruction on every proper occasion, and seeking to make every occasion of meeting fellow-mortals who are in danger of losing their souls, a proper one to show what they should do to be saved ; 7th—An earnest endeavor, as an assistant of the "good shepherd," to seek for the wandering and spiritually lost, and bring them into the fold (the church), as Jesus has assured us that "joy shall be in heaven over one sinner that repenteth, more than over ninety-and-nine just persons that need no repentance." [Luke xv, 7]; 8th—Keeping holy one-seventh part of the time, by adopting as a proper comment on the fourth commandment, the 13th and 14th verses of the lviii. chapter of Isaiah; 9th—A determination to obey the Lord's will (without waiting for a rich society to offer a bountiful salary,) by seeking to make the gospel known to the ignorant, and its restraining and elevating influences felt by those who are out of the way of salvation.

The most notable example of a failure to secure the promised reward for faithfulness in christian duties was that of one of the disciples of Jesus whom He ordained by His own personal authority as an apostle, Judas Iscariot, who from a lust of gain betrayed his Master, and has been a standing warning to bishops, presbyters and deacons, and indeed to all christians, that they use all diligence to continue the Christ's faithful soldiers and servants to their lives' end.

In conclusion, I will emphasize the article by quoting the Lord's words: "Watch ye therefore, for ye know not when the Master . . . . . cometh, ... lest coming suddenly he find you sleeping ; and what I say unto you (the ministers), I say unto all (the people), Watch."

ARTICLE XVII.

The Rich Young Man.—Matt. xix, 16—24; Mark x, 17—27; Luke xviii, 18—27.

THE person who came to Jesus and asked the important practical question: "What good thing shall I do, that I may have eternal life?" appeared to have been sincere and earnest, and to have had, to a considerable degree, a just conception of the importance of eternal life. He seemed also, to have had a very great respect for Jesus, which he manifested by the lowly act of kneeling to Him in an act of worship.

There is nothing to indicate that the young came with only the promptings of mere curiosity, to ascertain what Jesus would say upon the subject, in order to compare it with the teachings of the priests, who were the authorized expounders of the Levitical laws, and the scribes and Pharisees, who were supposed to be well instructed, both in the theory and practice of God's requirements; but he appears to have come to our Lord with a feeling that he could receive from Him more definite and satisfactory instructions as to what was really necessary to be done in order to secure life eternal, than was to be learned from the common sources of instruction in the community in which he lived.

The man was a ruler (probably of some synagogue,) in the coast of Judea beyond Jordan, therefore a little out from the center of religious influence, but yet near enough to be considerably influenced by it, and had some authority in the management of religious exercises on the Sabbath-days, perhaps similar to that now exercised by trustees, stewards and vestrymen in the religious societies of the present day. That being his position, we are warranted in believing that he was qualified to judge of the importance of securing a blessed life after the death of the body.

Perhaps in estimating the importance which this man may have attached to this subject, we should consider what are the ideas which the holy scriptures of the old testament give in regard to eternal life, and contrast it with what the same scriptures teach is to be the condition of those who fail to attain it, as he was familiar with their teachings. He had doubtless, learned from the book of Genesis (ii, 17) that God had threatened our first parents that in the day they disobeyed the one command which He gave them for a test of their love and gratitude, they should die; he had learned that the threatened death was not the death of the body, and he may have been taught that what they suffered as a consequence of their transgression was the loss of the favor of God, so that their condition was a state of continual suffering, and their experience was such as to show them that their "life was not worth living"—or as a marginal note explains, the original Hebrew is "dying thou shalt die,"—which may mean that the enjoyments of life which their souls and bodies were created to experience, would be denied them, and that they in reality should be dying while they lived in suffering, and at length it would end in a cessation of the life of the body; he may have learned from the book of Daniel [xii, 2] that at a future time "many of them that sleep in the dust of the earth shall awake some to everlasting life, and some to shame *and* everlasting contempt." And as Jesus, before that time had preached the same doctrine [see John v, 28, 29,] it may have been possible that the young man may have heard him, or had heard of his teaching on the subject. He may be supposed to have thought that the blessing of eternal life consisted of a never-ending existence of enjoyment, and that to be deprived of it was to be doomed to everlasting suffering; therefore we may perceive the reasons he had for anxiety, and for making earnest inquiry as to the best method of obtaining the one and avoiding the other.

But notice the form in which he asks the question: "Good master [teacher,] what good thing shall I do," etc. He seems to have had the notion that by doing some one thing, perhaps by building a synagogue for some destitute locality or a hospital, or some specific beneficent act, he could, once for all, make sure of and fit himself for the enjoyment of the blessing he sought, and then go on selfishly using his remaining wealth without any further concern, doing, as it were, a work of such a supererogatious merit that future shortcomings should be at least balanced by it.

In order to show the young man what his real religious state was, Jesus enquires first, why he calls Him good, stating that, in the full sense of the word, God is the only one who is perfectly good; and then with the very natural direction, he assures him that it is necessary to keep the commandments. Seeming not to comprehend that Jesus meant, he asked Him: "Which?" thinking, perhaps, that some more intricate and less common laws than the decalogue may have been meant. But when he is informed that those old commandments were the rules by which his life was to be tested and his claim to eternal life made secure, he seemed to be in a measure relieved of his anxiety, and confidently asserted that he had kept them from his youth up, and then, with an almost triumphant air, he asked: "What lack I yet?" The Master told him that something more is needed for him to do, that he may attain perfection, and in order to enable him to understand what was necessary, told him that, if he would sell his property for the benefit of the poor, he should "have treasure in heaven," and further directed that he should become His follower. This was a most astounding requirement to this young man; though he does not seem to question Jesus' right to require it —it was as if he had said to him, (according to idea of a learned commentator,): "Thou sayest thou hast kept God's law. Then thou art willing to do it still. Let thy obedience be put to the proof. God's law says 'thou shalt have no other Gods but Me.' Hast thou no other god? Hast thou not made a god of thy riches? Is not covetousness idolatry? Go, and cast down this idol, then thou mayest claim to obey at least one commandment. God, by his providence has given thee wealth; I, whom thou acknowledgest to be a teacher come from God, by His authority I instruct thee how to use it; and further require thee to follow Me, and I will teach thee thy future duty."

This seeker after eternal life seemed greatly disappointed—seemed to have set a greater value on the wealth which he possessed, than on the privilege of an eternal existence of peace and joy, and so he went away sorrowing, because he was so intoxicated with the earthly pleasures which his great possessions seemed to promise him for a few years, that they out-weighed, in his estimation, the everlasting happiness for which he had seemingly been so anxious to secure. And what a contrast between them!—never-ending joys without alloy on the one hand, and on the other a short period of pleasure mixed with much anxiety and disappointment, to be followed by everlasting shame and contempt.

It might be interesting to contemplate the probabilites of this man's future career, if he had followed Jesus' direction and become his disciple. He was evidently a well educated man, and a man of activity and energy, and also of such a character that Jesus loved him; and if he had accompanied the Redeemer, during the remainder of His earthly life, heard His instructions and witnessed His miracles, and though he might have been discouraged, (as were all the apostles,) at His crucifixion and death, he would doubtless have been re-assured by the resurrection, subsequent teachings and and ascension, he might, as he would have had superior advantages to St. Paul, in the earthly instructions of the Great Teacher, both before and after the the resurrection, have become as efficient a promoter of Christianity as was that great apostle,—if not more so, and therefore have received the gratitude and admiration of the good and great of the Church since that time, as well as the blessing and favor of Him who has promised those who are "faithful unto death" . . . a crown of life," [Rev. ii, 10.] But now he is only remembered as the rich young man who declined the call of Jesus to a great and glorious career in this life, and through that failure to do his duty probably lost the prize for which he had been so earnestly seeking, through the "deceitfulness of riches," [Matt. xiii, 22.]

Very pertinent and thrilling must have been the remarks of the Savior: "How hard is it for them that trust in riches to enter into the kingdom of God, etc. [Mark x, 24, 25.] And in the 29th and 30th verses assures His disciples that "There is no man that hath left house, or brethren, and sisters, or father or mother, or wife or children and lands for my sake and the gospel's, but shall receive a hundred fold now in this time, ... with persecutions; and in the world to come eternal life."

King Saul in his whole public career is a case where a very promising beginning, by repeated violations of God's commands, brought upon himself trouble and disaster, occasioned by the withdrawal of the favor of God. I Sam. x, 25—26 give an account of his prosperous beginning. xii., 5—15 make known the terms upon which continued prosperity was to be expected. xiii, 5—16 relates the beginning of his troubles. The xv chapter gives an instance of his disobedience. xviii, 7, shows the awakening of a wicked jealousy; and the chapters that follow to the xxxist contain the accounts of the numerous exhibitions of that jealousy; and the xxxist tells of his final overthrow.

A Rt. Reverend commentator on II Tim. iv, 5, says: "Evangelists did not form a separate order of the ministry. Eusebius speaks of large numbers of the early believers: 'They first fulfilled the saving injunction, in distributing their goods to the poor, then traveling abroad they fulfiled the work of Evangelists, being ambitious to preach Christ to those who had never heard of Him, and to deliver to them the text of the Holy Gospel.'—[Eusebius iii, 37.] So now a layman does not go beyond his measure in preaching the Gospel of Christ. What he may *not* do is to assume to administer the Sacraments."

ARTICLE XVIII.

The Two Sons.—Matt. xxi, 28—31.

PERHAPS there is no feeling more generally indulged in by youthful minds, than that their parents are disposed to be unreasonably strict with them in their demands, both in respect to the restrictions which they impose on the pastimes and desires of their young hearts, but also respecting those employments which conduce to the welfare of the family, and in which they may reasonably expect to share with the rest of the household. They too often regard anything that they do in obedience to the commands of their parents as a sort of supererogatory work, which by strict justice they are under no obligations to perform. They are apt to lose sight of the fact that, to their parents, under God, they owe their life, their present comforts and their future well-being, and that, therefore, when they have done all that they can do for their father and mother during their legal minority, they are still indebted to them. The writer remembers that, more than sixty years ago, he overheard his mother make the remark, "the only way that children can pay for their own bringing up, is to bring up children themselves;" and my own experience fully justifies the sentiment.

It is surely a fact that parents are under most sacred obligations to do all they can to prepare their children for a useful and successful life—see to it that their physical constitution is placed on as good a foundation as may be, and to correct as far as possible any hereditary imperfections they may have transmitted to them; to take care that their intellectual, moral and religious training is such as to best fit them to perform the duties which may devolve upon them toward the succeeding generation; and to be always ready to give them the best advice their own experience enables them to impart, in any circumstances in which their children may be unable to decide for themselves as to the wisest course to pursue.

But these obligations do not in the least modify or impair the duty of children "to love, honor and succor their father and mother," unless such parents have been criminally negligent of the duties which God has enjoined upon them. In fact the obligations of the parents in regard to their children only intensifies the duty of the children to give an implicit obedience to the requirements of a father or mother.

The parable of the two sons, which Jesus spake, was evidently intended to rebuke the leaders of the Jewish people for their opposition to Him and His doctrines, and to encourage those of the disreputable classes of the people who repented of their sins and believed and obeyed the gospel. I design in this article to pass over this branch of the subject with but short allusions, remarking that the class of people existing at the present time to whom the rebuke may apply, are those who make loud professions of willingness to work in the vineyard of the Lord (the Christian Church); are reasonably attentive to the public services of religion; but when called upon to make self-denying efforts for the spread of the gospel, are found to be negligent of their duty in regard to others, and slack in the private exercises of repentance and faith toward God and love to mankind for the Lord's sake. And those may be encouraged by it, who, while they sincerely acknowledge themselves to be miserable sinners, do works meet for repentance, and show, by their actions, that they thankfully accept the grace of God, and obediently keep His holy will and commandments.

But the main object of this article is to enforce the duty of minor children to obey their parents in all things that do not conflict with their duties to God— that is, if a parent should command a child to pay divine honors to a heathen god, or to bow down and worship an image or likeness, or take the name of God in vain, or do unnecessary work on the day set apart for rest and religious worship, or commit a murder, or adultery, or steal, or tell a lie, or wish so much for what belongs to another that he or she would be willing to take unlawful means to get it, or do any other act plainly contrary to the laws of God,—in those cases it would be no violation of the fifth commandment to decline to do the parents bidding; the children would thereby show that they were actuated by the high religious principle of obedience to the highest authority. But the refusal of obedience should be made in respectful language, and with sorrow that they have been asked to do anything contrary to God's laws.

The parable supposes that a father says to a son: "son, go work to-day in my vineyard." But the son, probably feeling that his father's command so seriously interfered with his own plans for the day that, in his disappointment he impetuously dissents, by plainly declaring: "I will not." But after reflection on the matter, he concludes that he has done wrong in refusing to obey his father, he changes his mind, and by his actions shows his repentance and obedience; for although the refusal was a highly reprehensible insult to his father, his after-obedience in a great measure atoned for it so much so that the father was, perhaps, as much gratified with his behavior, as if he had at the first consented and then performed his duty in the matter.

But the father has another son to whom he makes the same command, and from him receives a ready reply of: "I go sir," but he did not go. It may be that many times, a boy who makes such a ready aquiescence to his parent's command, intends to fulfill his promise, but after temptations—opportunities for pleasurable enjoyments occur, and trusting to his parent's clemency he violates his promise, and thus incurs a deeper guilt than he would, had he at first declined to obey—not only failing to obey the command, but failing to keep his engagement. And on other occasions a child may make such a promise while not intending to fulfill it; in such a case the child acts the hypocrite in the first instance and in the last falsifies his word, both of which sins are of a deeper degree of heinousness than either of the two previously supposed cases. The teaching of the parable is that the son first mentioned was the least sinner against his father.

Bearing on this subject, I think I cannot do better than to make an extract from a book entitled: "The New Whole Duty of Man," written probably over 200 years ago, which descended to my family from three previous generations of the ancestors of my wife, and is now in the keeping of the fifth generation. I copy from the 21st edition, printed in 1770. On the 201st page may be read:

"The next duty that children owe to their parents is *Obedience*. Children obey your parents in the Lord; for this is right and well-pleasing, unto the Lord. This is a certain principle: while children want understanding to direct their choice and will, they should have no will but that of their parents; and therefore should obey, till arrived at more sound judgment. Parents must be allowed to discern what is most proper for their children; and though they be now and then mistaken yet it is always safest to follow their commands and instructions whose main end and purpose is to do them good. Nothing can be plainer, than that parents love their children dearly and without design, and are older, wiser and more experienced, and the fittest to command and to be obeyed by their children; and for this reason God, to show how fit it is to obey our parents, calls himself our Father, and from that relation calls for our obedience likewise. Let then stubborn, headstrong children consider the ties they have to be obedient to their parents, and they will find both pleasure and security in being so; the approbation of all, and the blessing of God goes with it; whereas nothing but trouble of mind, sorrow, shame, infamy and the displeasure of Almighty God, attend disobedience to their good and wholesome commands. But, if the command of a parent is to do evil, or requires a child to lie, or steal, or to do any other act by which the laws of God are broken, he must prefer his duty to God; for we must obey God rather than man."

That it may be seen how the Lord regarded, (and of course still regards,) disobedience to parents, I will quote a few passages: "And he that curseth his father and his mother, shall surely be put to death." [Exod. xxi, 17.] Heathen nations in ancient times conceded to parents the rights to take the lives of their children; but to the children of Israel God allowed it only after formal trial and condemnation by the civil authority, on complaint of the father and mother. [See Deut. xxi, 18—21; also xxvii, 16.]

Read what Jesus said to those who found fault with

THE TWO SONS. 107

Him and His disciples, because they neglected some ceremonial observances which they held by traditions: "Why do you also transgress the commandment of God, by your tradition? For God commanded, saying: Honor thy father and mother; and he that curseth his father or mother, let him die the death, but ye say, Whoever shall say to *his* father or *his* mother, *It is* a gift, by whatsoever thou mightest be profited by me; and honor not his father or his mother, *he shall be free;* Thus have ye made the commandment of God of none effect by your tradition."—[Matt. xv, 3—6,] and the same lesson is taught in Mark vii, 9—13.

Turn now to a more cheerful passage, which is both a command and a promise: "Honor thy father and thy mother: that thy days may be long upon the land, which the Lord thy God giveth thee"—[Exod. xx, 12.]

A case in bible history which illustrates the evil of disobedience of children to parents, was the sons of Eli, the high priest, whose position was such that, had he lived in modern times, he would be styled the primate of Israel; [see I Samuel ii, 22—25; 27—34; iii, 10—14; iv, 12—22.]

We may with profit contrast the history of the sons of Eli with that of the great boy-preacher Samuel; he was a remarkably obedient boy, whose first sermon may be found in the first book of Samuel, iii, 11—14; and he was immediately recognized as a prophet of the Lord by the people of the whole nation. In after life he became the chief Judge and administrator of the laws of God, and as such was entitled to as much respect as the greatest doctor of divinity and doctor of laws of these days.

ARTICLE XIX.

THE WICKED HUSBANDMEN.—Matt. xxi, 33—44;
Mark xii, 1—11; Luke xx, 9—18.

THIS parable was intended to reprove the rulers of the nation of Israel for their failure to pay the appointed rental to the Lord, for the use of the privileges and fruits of the vineyard, meaning by it, the observance of the acts of worship prescribed by the Levitical laws, and a tenth of the income of the people to be devoted to the religious institutions of the country. Jesus charges them with persecuting the faithful preachers which God had sent to warn them of the consequences of their unfaithfulness, and urge them to the performance of their duties, and informs them that they may expect that He will take the vineyard from them and give it to another nation—even as they had judged that the householder, "the lord of the vineyard . . . . will miserably destroy those wicked men, and will let out *his* vineyard to other husbandmen which shall render him the fruits in their season."

It is often the case in the affairs of this life that persons become so intoxicated with desires to keep what they have in possession, that they will by bold scheming make attempts to retain what rightfully belongs to others, but are frustrated by some miscarriage of their plans, and they find that even in dealings with their fellows, they are not able to succeed in their attempts, and like the husbandmen of the parable, they discover that they have miserably failed, and instead of succeeding in their schemes find themselves deprived of the hopes that they might reasonably have expected had they honestly fulfilled their obligations. How much greater must be the degree of infatuation or intoxication which those are possessed by, who fancy that they can withhold from the God of the Universe His rightful claims, for the use of the privileges which He is continually bestowing upon them, and yet escape in the final judgment, the penalties he has declared in the bible that He will visit upon those who are ungrateful for His gifts, disobey His commandments and deny His authority.

In the gradual manner, by slow degrees, by which our minds are opened to terrestrial things, we do not as fully appreciate what God has prepared for us in the arrangements by which we are surrounded, as we may suppose that Adam and Eve may have been able to have done, when, possessed of the full strength of body and mind they found themselves in the garden of Eden, as with pure and holy thoughts they surveyed the beauty which they saw about them, and experienced the convenient arrangements which God had made for their sustenance and pleasure and employment. They saw the delicious fruits upon the trees, they perceived the aromatic flavors of the flowers and the vegetation which covered the vines—all beautiful to the sight, all delightful to the smell, all pleasant to the taste; every thing in its primeval freshness and vigor of growth—nothing wilted, withered or dead; surely the gratitude which must have filled their hearts for so bountiful and luxurious provisions for their comfort and happiness, would have overflowed in acts of worship and adoration, in resolutions of obedience, and expressions of astonishment and admiration.

In the case of Adam's and Eve's descendants, the knowledge comes to us so gradually, through the imperfections of vision, the failure to apprehend them and the inability to comprehend them, until many years of experience enables us to get a partial knowledge of what the Lord has provided, and is providing for us; and then, too, so many of these things appear to us to be produced and arranged by ourselves, that we are very liable to forget that our powers to plan and perform and to appreciate and enjoy come from our Creator and Preserver, so that in strictness of speech they may be said to be his gifts, while we are but the instruments by which he supplies them to us and to our children.

We shall better understand what our Lord meant, if we refer to the original law which He charged the Jews with violating, which is as follows: "And all the tithe of the land *whether* of the seed of the land, *or* of the fruit of the tree, *is* the Lord's; *it is* holy unto the Lord." [Leviticus xxvii, 30. The directions as to how it was to be observed may be found in Deuteronomy xii, 5—14; and in I. Chronicles, xxiii, 27—32.

The prophets of old whom the Lord sent to remind His chosen people of their duties, were not negligent in giving instructions on both the subjects of worship and tithes, as may be seen from the following passages: "The ways of Zion do mourn, because none come to her solemn feasts; all her gates are desolate; her priests sigh, her virgins are afflicted, and she is in bitterness. Her adversaries are the chief, her enemies prosper; for the Lord hath afflicted her for the multitude of her transgressions; her children are gone into captivity before the enemy. And from the daughter of Zion all her beauty is departed; her princes are become like harts *that* find no pasture, and they are gone without strength before the pursuer. Jerusalem remembered in the days of her affliction and of her miseries all her pleasant things in the days of old, when her people fell into the hand of the enemy, and none did help her; the adversaries saw her *and* did mock at her sabbaths. [Lamentations of Jeremiah i, 4—7.]

Another prophet, speaking in the name of the Lord, said to another generation 200 years later: "Even from the days of your fathers ye are gone away from mine ordinances and have not kept *them*. Return unto me and I will return unto you, saith the Lord of Hosts. . . . Ye are cursed with a curse; for ye have robbed Me, *even* this whole nation." He then makes gracious promises conditioned upon their return to their duty, as follows: " Bring ye all the tithes into the storehouse, that there may be meat in My house, and prove Me now herewith,. saith the Lord of Hosts, if I will not open you the windows of Heaven and pour you out a blessing, *there shall not be room* enough *to receive it.* And I will rebuke the devourer for your sakes, and he shall not destroy the fruits of your ground; neither shall your vine cast her fruit before the time in the field, saith the Lord of Hosts. And all nations shall call you blessed; for ye shall be a delightsome land, saith the Lord of hosts." [Malachi iii, 7, 9—12.]

As to the proportion of time and product which the laws of Moses enjoined, can one seventh part of our time be an unreasonable amount to be devoted to the honor and glory of the Being from whom we derive our bodies and souls, our mental and moral endowments, our health and comforts, when it is so evident that the rest from physical labor which results from it is really a benefit to us physically, morally and religously? and as to the proportion of the increase which we derive from God's gifts, is not a tenth a proper amount to be set apart for the compensation of those whom He entrusts the carrying on of the work of extending the knowledge of His name, the revelation of His character and the supremacy of His laws, when these services afford the best security for the truest happiness while this life lasts, and the greatest assurance that the future life of those who love and obey the Lord, will be restful, joyous and everlasting?

Perhaps we may, in the light of the subsequent history, both of the Children of Israel and the Disciples of Christ, assume that Jesus meant that the privileges of the vineyard should be given to all of every nation who should become His true followers. It is very evident that, since that time, the nations that have had the chief controlling influence among civilized peoples have been christian nations, while the Children of Israel have been scattered into various countries of the world.

Had the Jews as a people, after the resurrection and ascension of Jesus, become convinced, as was their Governor Pilate, that He was without fault, and many of their notable men, that He was their promised Messiah, and had accepted His atonement for their sins and followed His teachings, would not their subsequent history have been far different from what it has been? It is reasonable to suppose that they would have been obedient to the temporal rule of the Romans and so escaped the destruction of their temple and their city; that they would have cherished in their hearts a love for all mankind—even their enemies, doing good to those who hated them, and praying for those who persecuted them, and proving that they were the children of Him who "maketh His sun to rise on the evil and on the good and sendeth rain on the just and the unjust." [Matt. v, 44, 45.] Had they done this it is probable that they would have remained in undisturbed possession of their own land, would have won the love of the Gentiles, and in process of time the City of Jerusalem would have been the capital of the christian world. Indeed, it has been the ambition of many christian nations to gain possession of the land given by the Lord to Abraham and his seed, in order that it might be inhabited by a people who would obey the ten commandments given on Mount Sinai to Moses, and the land where Jesus taught His Gospel and performed His mighty works.

Let us who acknowledge ourselves to be the bond-servants of Jesus, examine the habits of our lives, whether we faithfully spend a seventh part of our time in acts of holy worship and holy living—not as an unpleasant task but as a loving service; and do we devote a tenth of our income to the maintaining and enlarging Christ's kingdom on the earth?

St. Paul declares to the Corinthians, [I Cor. vi, 19, 20]: "Ye are not your own; for ye are bought with a price; therefore glorify God in your body, and in your spirit which are God's." And the same apostle, who as Saul the Israelite was a most zealous maintainer of the Mosaic observances, but as Paul the Christian he preached the gospel earnestly, and warned the Christians at Rome,(I quote from the revised version,): "God did not cast off His people which He foreknew. Or wot ye not what the scripture saith of Elijah? how he pleadeth with God against Israel; Lord they have killed Thy prophets, they have digged down thine altars: and I am left alone, and they seek my life. But what saith the answer of God unto him? I have left for myself seven thousand men, who have not bowed the knee to Baal. Even so, at this present time also, there is a remnant according to the election of grace. . . . . . By their unbelief they were broken off, and thou standest by faith. Be not highminded but fear; for if God spared not the natural branches, neither will He spare thee. Behold then the goodness and severity of God; towards them that fell severity; but toward thee goodness, if thou continue in *His* goodness; otherwise thou also shalt be cut off.—[Rom. xi, 2—5, 20—22.

This is true of Christians of all times, and everywhere. It is of the greatest importance that we carefully ponder these truths. American Christians should heed these warnings for they are no more likely to escape the destiny of being broken off than were the Israelites for their unbelief, nor than were the Romans, if they failed in their duty to God, of being cut off.

God, in His dealings with mankind, treats them according their faith or lack of it—those who trust in Him and show it by obedience, will find that He is merciful and gracious; but those who despise Him and hate His laws and oppose his sincere worshippers, or seek by artifice to draw His disciples from their allegiance to Him, will find that in the end, their plans for robbing God of his righteous demands will miserably fail, and that others will succeed to the enjoyment of the blessings of His vineyard (the Church), who will be more faithful in making proper returns for the blessings which He bestows upon them.

In the allusions which Jesus made to the rejected corner stone, He is understood to teach that those who reject him will be disappointed in their best prospects in this life, and at the resurrection, the finally impenitent will experience, in the sentence of the Judge, a grinding to powder, as it were, of their hopes, which until that time they may have cherished, of final happiness.

Since writing the foregoing I have seen a comment on the last-mentioned passage which I copy, as follows: "The meaning is: This great and general revelation of the will God, by the Messiah, being the last discovery that He will ever make to mankind; whoever shall stumble and be offended at any part of it, or behave himself in any manner unworthy of it, shall be severely punished. But he that shall utterly and finally reject it, or behave himself so as to deserve the utmost effect of the wrath which it reveals and brings along with it, shall be miserably and utterly destroyed."

D'Oyley and Mant's Commentary, American edition.

ARTICLE XX.

THE UNSYMPATHETIC NEIGHBORS. Luke xiv, 16—24.

AN invitation to an entertainment or festival is usually thought to be a matter of considerable importance both by the inviters and the invited—by the inviters, lest they should omit some whom they ought to invite, or invite some who would be regarded as unworthy to associate with their friends; and by the candidates for invitations, lest they should be forgotten or passed over by those whom they regard as only equals, and therefore think themselves entitled to an invitation by the ordinary rules of social etiquette; and if by any cause an expected one fails to be received, it is the occasion of much disappointment, and it may be of heart-burnings and future estrangements.

I next present another parable spoken by Jesus. The title of the parable is: "The Great Supper." The maker of the supper is a man,—probably the principal man of the vicinity. In previous remarks [verses 12—14] Jesus had been teaching that Christians should not invite their personal friends and rich neighbors, to their festal entertainments, but in an unselfish manner call the poor, the maimed, the lame and the blind, and they would be blessed of God; and at the resurrection of the just their recompense would be received from a higher source, and at a time when it would be beyond the power of their equals in society to do them any good.

The statement that the supper was "great" indicates that it was something more than an ordinary evening repast—enough to satisfy the requirements of the body after the labors of the day; but was furnished in great profusion with a great variety of rare and costly viands and beverages, calculated to tempt the appetite to unwonted indulgence. The invitations were numerous, and probably included all persons of any notoriety in the community—land-holders, merchants, manufacturers, professional men, capitalists and officers of the government; in fine, a very select class of persons. We may readily conceive what cause the host had for being offended when they all declined his hospitality. He doubtless felt very much chagrined by the covert insults which their behavior implied.

The parable sets forth very definitely the excuses which men make for neglecting the gospel.

We notice that there is an apparent show of civility by the apologetic excuses that were given, and we may consider the three excuses as only samples of a larger number. The first said "I have bought a field and must needs go out and see it;" he may have been a young man just commencing life and making his first effort to secure a homestead. The second may have been a little farther advanced having secured a farm and was making preparations to cultivate it; and so he must test the capabilities of his ten oxen. The third had probably obtained a home, and was making the crowning effort of his ambition by introducing his wife to the home he had prepared. But, whatever their condition may have been, they are all agreed in slighting the civilities of their rich neighbor, and so lost the aid that would have resulted from his friendship.

When it became certain that the people who had been invited declined the honor of being guests on the occasion, the host made a sudden resolve that he would not be frustrated in his designed hospitality, and so he sent his servant out into the streets and lanes to bring in another class of people who would be sure to come, and who would appreciate the honor of an invitation, and were in a condition to enjoy the good things provided by the generous citizen; and when it was discovered that there was room for more, the servant was sent out into the highways and hedges to induce all he found to come and enjoy the supper.

By this time, we may suppose the master of the house had overcome his feelings of chagrin and disappointment, and was taking an interest in learning the circumstances of his new guests, and giving them profitable advice as to their future conduct, perhaps promising future aid to those who were worthy and were in need of assistance; while the guests were cheering each other and their entertainer with their manifestations of sociability, comfort and gratitude. It would be natural to imagine that after such a supper was over, such guests would not be disposed to criticize it, or the deportment of their host, or make comparisons of his treatment of one over the others; and in the after meetings, with him, their manifestations of respect and honor toward him would be likely to be marked, by greater sincerity and reverence. The man himself might discover that he had new sources of happiness in ministering to the wants of his poor neighbors, and witnessing the improvements in their comfort which his beneficence and counsel enabled them to enjoy with thankfulness.

Many who think it wise to neglect the warnings and invitations of the servants of the Lord till they have acquired a certain degree of worldly success, seem to be unaware of the well-proved fact that religious duties and thoughts, interspersed with lawful, worldly avocations, will serve to cheer their lives, by lessening the disagreeable effects of disappointments, and even render welcome the approach of the sleep of death, which may truly be regarded as a messenger to summon true Christians away from the toils and trials of mortality, to enter upon the rest that remaineth for the people of God.

See also [Matt. vi, 31—33.] Christ's instruction on this point in the greatest sermon ever preached.

ARTICLE XXI.

THE FOOLISH VIRGINS.—Matt. xxv, 1—13.

THE parable of the wise and foolish virgins, is one in which Jesus makes a comparison between those who are careful to provide for the future of their religious experience, and those who merely act upon the impulses at the time presented to their minds.

As this article is mainly designed to impress upon the reader the unwisdom of possessing the character represented by the foolish virgins, I shall have little to remark about the wise ones.

Of the word "Fool," from which the adjective foolish is derived, there have been four different significations given: 1. A person destitute of reason—an idiot, etc.; persons of this class are not held to be accountable for their actions; 2. Persons deficient in judgment or who act contrary to the dictates of wisdom—the class to which the foolish virgins belong; they not being wicked or vicious, but not careful for the future, and neglecting to make provision for the possible necessities of a coming emergency; 3. One who acts contrary to moral and religious wisdom—a wicked person; 4. One who counterfeits folly—a professional jester.

An examination of the preceding chapter will show that it contains Jesus' answer to the question of the disciples: " What *shall be* the sign of thy coming and the end of the world?" and this chapter commences with the word "then," which indicates that it is a continuation of the same discourse upon what may be expected at the end of the world.

The ten virgins represent all christians who are expecting the second coming of Christ—the bridegroom; they all took their lamps well filled with oil, which they probably thought would last till the time the bridegroom was expected to meet them. But, as it often happens, previous calculations by those who do not know all the circumstances attending a festal occasion, were not realized by the event, and the delay was prolonged beyond all the expectations of these girls; they became tired of waiting while the bridegroom tarried; they sat down by the wayside and finally fell asleep. This sleep is supposed to represent the sleep of death,* which all must experience, except those who may be alive at the second coming of Christ, who, we are informed, will be changed from natural bodies to spiritual bodies, in "the twinkling of an eye at the last trump."—[I. Cor. xv, 51, 52.]

The oil in the vessels represents good works which

---

* The foregoing opinion of what is signified by the sleep of the virgins, is the one that seems most satisfactory to my mind, keeping in view that it is part of the answer to the question as to what will take place at the "end of the world." The following is the opinion which I relied upon:

"'They all slumbered and slept.' To understand this of growing careless (as some do) † seems to destroy, or at least greatly weaken the force of the parable, which lies in the fact that, while *some* did grow careless, the others continued in readiness to the end. It is better to understand this verse as describing the falling asleep one after another of wise and foolish alike in the sleep of death. It thus teaches that, as our state of preparation is when we fall asleep in death, so will it be when we awake at the resurrection."—*Rt. Rev. Dr. How, Bishop of Bedford, England.*

The two following extracts seem not to disagree with Dr. How, though they do not state so definitely what the sleep signifies:

"The sleep of all the virgins is alike necessary to the imagery of the parable. The bridegroom is to come suddenly and without notice to all. . . . . . The watchfulness of the wise virgins consisted not in knowing when the bridegroom was coming but in being prepared when He came suddenly."—*Canon Cook, of Exeter, England.*

"Neither is the *falling asleep* of the virgins intended to be specially significant; for as it happened in the case of the exemplary wise as well, it cannot represent any moral short-coming."—*H. A. W. Meyer, Th. D., Germany.*

---

† The following passage is from an old preacher (1680) who had a different opinion.

. . . . "They all slumbered and slept—this did the wise virgins as well as the foolish. Thus, too often, even the best and most considerate sort of Christians are not so watchful as they ought to be, to prepare for death and judgment."—*Rt. Rev. Dr. Tillotson, Archbishop of Canterbury, England.*

are the results of repentance towards God and faith in the Lord Jesus, through whose merits, past sins are forgiven, and by the aid of the Holy Ghost the christian graces of love, joy, peace, long-suffering, gentleness, goodness, faith, meekness, temperance, are cherished and practised.

When the summons came that the bridegroom was coming, the foolish virgins discovered that their lamps burned with only a flickering light indicating that the oil was gone. The words translated "are gone out" are more literally rendered "are going out." [See Revised Version.] In their extremity they apply to the wise virgins for a portion of their oil, but the wise ones, in their fears lest they should need all they had, declined; by this statement, Jesus is understood to teach us that we cannot safely rely upon the virtues of others to supply our own lack of preparation for an admission to the marriage feast of the Son of God, but that the only preparation that will avail us will be a love for and a practise of holiness in the heart.

Perhaps the difference between Christians who are represented by the wise virgins and those represented by the foolish ones, may be: the one is really devout in heart—striving to conform their lives, both inwardly and outwardly—in thoughts, desires and actions, to the rules of God's commandments—giving up their own wishes whenever they come in conflict with what they believe to be God's will; while the other are only religious in outward appearance, conforming to the customs of religious society, mainly for the standing they expect it will give them in their earthly relations —with no real love for that holiness of heart which is necessary to enjoy the presence of God and the Christ of God, and of the holy angels and of the people whom God has sanctified and made holy.

THE FOOLISH VIRGINS.

If the foregoing interpretations are correct, are not many "who profess and call themselves Christians" in great danger of discovering, too late, that when their bodies are awakened to life at the coming of Christ at "the end of the world," they will be unprepared to join the procession which is to accompany the bridegroom to the marriage supper of the Lamb.

What is the cause of the mistake which those professed Christians make who are represented by the foolish virgins? Evidently, they think so much of the pleasures and employments and riches of the world, that they come to a conclusion in their own minds, that a certain amount of outward religious observances will be all that the Lord requires of them; while the main object of their ambition is, to stand high in the estimation of their associates in the world; they banish from their thoughts the important truth that God looketh at the heart, and demands the supreme love of His creatures for Himself; and they live on, allowing the pleasures and ambitions of the world to intoxicate their minds and divert them from what is the great object which He proposes for our existence, viz: to glorify Him on earth, and enjoy Him forever in Heaven.

If these things are so, it is a very serious matter; and it is of the utmost importance that all should strive with all their power to work out their "salvation with fear and trembling," remembering, that they will surely fail unless God shall work in them "both to will and to do of *His* good pleasure." [Phil. ii, 12, 13.] Unless they do this, they put in jeopardy their future and everlasting welfare, and are in imminent danger of meeting the fate foreshadowed by the rejection of the foolish virgins of the parable.

A similar warning is given by Jesus, which was recorded by St. Luke, [see chapter xiii, 23—28.]

ARTICLE XXII.

THE WICKED AND SLOTHFUL SERVANT.—
Matt. xxv, 14—30.

THE parable of the talents is, like that of the ten virgins, one which only a part of it has a particular relation to the main object of these articles, viz: to make prominent the warnings in the bible, against yielding to the temptations which beset human nature to indulge in sins both of commission and omission, towards God and our fellow creatures.

The largest part of the parable relates to the good and faithful servants, but with them I shall have little to do except to refer to them by way of contrast to the course adopted by the wicked and slothful servant.

The first remark that I make respecting the word "servant" is that, in the Jewish economy, and generally in the Christian Scriptures, it means a bond-servant. There were various ways by which persons became bound to serve others—one way was by being a thief, and if he had nothing to make restitution he was to be sold for his theft, [see Ex. xxii, 3]; another way was by being in debt, when a person's services could be sold to pay it, but could not be sold for a longer term than six years; if the master had given a man-servant a wife and she has borne him sons or daughters, the wife and her children remained the master's, but he might go out free [Ex. xxi, 2, 4]; if the man-servant declared that he loved his wife and children, and refused to go out, the master should bring him to the judges and also bring him to the doorpost, and his master bored his ear through with an awl, and he must serve for ever, [Ex. xxi, 5, 6.]

We may presume that the slothful servant, (as was probably the case with the other servants,) was bound to this man by his own act and choice, and therefore under a sacred obligation to use both the powers of his body and mind to the best of his ability in the service of his master, which was more than the ordinary hired servant was expected to do, who generally only stipulated to serve with the skill and powers of his body, and only for the time which was agreed upon.

And so it is with Christians who have arrived at years of discretion. Having incurred debts which the efforts of a whole life can never pay; but the Savior has arranged for the payment of the indebtedness if they will turn from their sins and believe and obey Him, and use the talents which the Lord has given them for His honor and glory, which if faithfully performed, He will give the commendation of being "good and faithful servants," and invite them to participate in His "joy" which will never end.

And may it not be so with many of the human race, that they can be counted as thieves, if they have used the powers and faculties of their bodies and minds and the favorable circumstances with which the Providence of God has surrounded them, in merely self-indulgence, or worse still, in ministering to the moral depravity of their fellow-creatures, or yet more wickedly, have opposed the observance of God's laws—both those which have been written on their consciences and those which may be learned from the Holy Scriptures—and in giving aid to his enemies (the wicked angels) in their nefarious designs against the welfare of the human race? But even these the Lord will receive as servants, if they will cease their rebellion and accept pardon offered through the merits of the Christ, and relying on His aid will spend the remainder of their lives in sincere efforts to set their affections on their Creator, Preserver and Benefactor, and on the holy employments which are the results of gratitude and love.

When we interpret the parable as to its spiritual significations, as relating to events to take place at the end of the world, the man traveling into a far country, is understood to represent Jesus' bodily presence leaving the world at His ascension, and giving to His disciples the special abilities and graces, which if used faithfully, will enable them all to do something to advance the prosperity of His kingdom in the hearts of mankind.

It is stated that the two first-named servants traded with their money, probably by buying large quantities of articles (by wholesale, as we say,) and then selling them at an advance, so that at the return of the lord they had doubled the money; and in doing this they had to exercise prudence in purchasing, industry in selling, and care in investing the profits. This in its religious application may mean that the servants of the Lord Jesus whose abilities, whether mental or financial, enable them to exercise a large influence for the furtherance of the gospel in the world, if they use their abilities faithfully, either by preaching or supporting those who preach, or in any other way cause the gospel to be made known and accepted, will be acknowledged as faithful servants, and permitted to enter into the joy of the Lord, or while receiving the commendation of the Master will be permitted to enjoy the fruits of his industry in the improved resources for happiness, which the results of his previous labors had provided. And the same remark is applicable to the servant whose abilities were less—faithfulness in using them will secure the same reward.

The servant who received the one talent is understood to refer to those Christians of the lowest grade of intelligence, who, if they cannot become teachers or prominent exemplars of the christian life, may yet, by a humble walk in the religious course do something to cause those who observe them to think well of the principles and truths which make a simple and unlearned person so good a neighbor and friend. If the servant whose case we are considering had done this, he would have done what his matter reproved him for not doing—put the money "to the exchangers," (or as the revised version has it, "to the bankers,") when he would have received not only the talent, but added usury. The word "usury" at that time signified what money was worth to the user in doing business—equivalent to rent for the use of any other kind of property; at the present time it means a higher rate of interest than is allowed by the laws of a State, which many persons, taking advantage of a borrower's necessity, extort more than its use is worth; this is called extortion in the Scriptures, [I Cor. vi, 10.]

I now come to the amount of money entrusted to the slothful servant, which cannot be definitely stated, as a talent was a weight either of gold or silver. If it is reckoned as of silver, it may be sufficient for the purpose of this article to roughly estimate the value as equal to about one thousand dollars, which was a large sum to entrust to a servant of but moderate abilities.

What this unprofitable servant of the parable did was to bury the talent in the earth—letting it lie there of no use to any one; it were better it had been left in the mine, so far as its use during the time it was under the control of this slothful man was concerned.

The religious condition of professed christians, who are represented by the last-named servant, is that of persons who, though nominally reckoned among christian people, as having taken upon themselves the obligations of a christian life, yet perform none of its duties and do not exhibit in their lives any of its virtues, but, on the contrary, their lives are so filled with the affairs of this life, that no one who observes them can discover that they are the disciples of Christ whose great apostle to the Gentiles exhorted his followers to: "Be not conformed to this world." Or if they are known as having become the disciples of Christ, their habits of life are such as to repel their acquaintances from a proper consideration of claims of the Lord upon them.

What were the reasons for this servant's failure in duty? A right-minded person, we might naturally suppose, would have felt honored by the confidence which had been manifested in him, and sought to justify his master's choice by endeavoring to employ the capital entrusted to him in the best manner he was able, to advance the interests of the lord's family. The first reason may have been that he was "wicked"—he repudiated his master's claim for his services, and determined to shirk the duties which had been laid upon him; he had no love for his master or his family, and would make no effort to ensure their prosperity, although his own welfare was indissolubly bound up with their well-being. A second reason appears to have been that he was "slothful," or lazy—he had no disposition to make the exertions necessary to success, preferring to spend his time in the trivial round of the common-place employments of getting his food and raiment, and amusing himself as much as possible, with no care for the promotion of his master's interests. He may have argued in own mind that he was not capable of conducting the business which he had been ordered to undertake, and that if he should fail in it, and lose the money he would be severely blamed; therefore he concluded that the safest way for him to do was to make sure that it would not be lost. He seems not to have thought of putting it where others could have used it, and that in that way the lord might receive some benefit from the use of his capital; and by this lack of forethought his indolence of mind as well as of body, was shown.

The sentence passed upon this unfaithful man was: "Take therefore the talent from him . . . . . . and cast ye the unprofitable servant into outer darkness; there shall be weeping and gnashing of teeth."

In the course of the sentence a rule is given which teaches us that, if we make a diligent use of our abilities for the glory of God, by efforts to promote the influence the Gospel of Jesus, in the hearts and on the lives of mankind, we may expect the commendation of the Lord; but if we neglect to so use them, we have no promise of favor, but every reason to expect a disgraceful and miserable future.

JUDAS BETRAYING JESUS.

ARTICLE XXIII.

JUDAS ISCARIOT.—Matt. xxvi, 14—16, 47-50, xxvii, 3-5; Mark xiv, 10, 11, 18—21, 42—45; Luke xxii, 47—53; John xviii, 1—12.

IN several of the preceding articles I have given my attention to some of the parables spoken by Jesus the Christ, to illustrate the dealings of the Lord with people in various relations and under a variety of circumstances, and showing what may be expected to happen to some particular characters, as the result of their actions or a neglect of the proper activity to secure a desirable object. In this article I take up the subject of an actual historical fact, and one from which very important warnings can be derived.

Judas Iscariot, (or to designate him more correctly Judas of Karioth, probably a native of Karioth, a town in the tribe of Judah mentioned in the xv. of Joshua 25th,) to distinguish him from the person mentioned by St. Luke [vi, 16,] as Judas the brother of James, who was the writer of the epistle of Jude.

Of the early history of Judas Iscariot, we have no knowledge, except that his father's name was Simon, [John vi, 71]. The first mention of his name occurs in Matt. x, where is given an account of the choosing of the twelve apostles. Judas had, probably been a disciple for some time; but it is evident from the character of the notices of him, that in choosing to be a scholar of Jesus he acted from worldly motives. He had charge of what was given to his Master for the support of the Great Teacher and his pupils, and seemed to be particularly interested in having the most made of every thing which could be turned to a pecuniary advantage, [see John xii, 4—6]; this passage more than intimates that he was not very scrupulous as to the way in which he gained possession of what he carried in his bag, and also that he desired credit for a degree of benevolence which he did not possess.

Jesus showed that he knew what Judas' disposition was, [see John vi, 70]. It has been a great question among christian teachers as to the reasons why the Savior chose such a character for one of his chief ministers; for although Judas and others of the eleven may have chosen to become His disciples, it was He who chose them to be His original twelve apostles, and sent them forth to act in His name, and proclaim the good news. Probably a number of reasons were in his mind for the choice, and possibly the following may have been among them: He would by that fact, give His followers in all future time to understand that they are not to expect perfection, or even freedom from hypocrisy, among His ministers, so that, while we are to listen to their preaching and practise the course of living which they prescribe so far as their teachings are founded upon the rules which the Christ has left us in His gospel; yet we are not unhesitatingly to follow their instructions, when their tendency is to lower the standard of christian living below the plain teachings of the scriptures; but we may use their ministrations for the promotion of our spiritual health, as, if they have been truly called by the Lord to His service, they do not act in their own names, but in the name and by the authority of their Master.

I now proceed to the consideration of the events leading to the act for doing which Judas has, ever since, been thought to have been the most wicked person who ever lived.

When, as St. Luke informs us, [xxii, 3,] Satan entered into Judas, he went to the chief priests and captains and offered to betray his Master to them. We may infer that these priests had made complaint to the Roman authorities, who had sent officers to arrest Jesus; but before they could do this, they must find where He was and be able to identify Him; as we should bear in mind that at that time there were thousands of strangers in Jerusalem, in attendance upon the feast of the passover commemoration. So the first prompting to the act was from Satan; and it was only because the temptation was addressed to a mind whose natural impulses were easily directed to any thing from which pecuniary gain could be derived that Satan was able to influence him. Had he promptly resisted the temptation, he might have become one whom Christians would have been proud to honor as a saint. And so, too, many who since that time have begun in the christian life, if they had resolutely resisted every impulse of their minds which they had reason to think was prompted by an evil spirit, they would have been able to withstand the wiles of the devils, and have been saved from back-sliding into perdition. As a most pertinent exhortation and direction on this point read Ephes. vi, 10—16.

Judas, after receiving the promise of a reward if he would deliver his Master to the authorities, suggested as the sign by which they would know Him that he would give Him the salutation which has ever been regarded as evincing the most tender affection and sincere love—a kiss, evidently designing to deceive all who witnessed the act into a belief that he was a true and faithful disciple and apostle; but how must he have felt reproved when the Master showed him that his hypocrisy was known and that his scheme to deceive had failed of its object.

Had Judas become satisfied that Jesus was deceiving the people, and from that consideration was induced to do what he could to stop His career, and for that purpose had secured the aid of the authorities to bring Him to justice, and had approached Him with an air of injured confidence and informed the officers that, that was the guilty man, his act would have been regarded with much less detestation than it has been; but when it is remembered that he came with the cheering words: "Hail, Master," and then saluted Him with an action of most confidential endearment, all for the purpose of pointing Him out to those who were intending to put Him to death, the act seems treacherous in a most aggravated degree.

No account is given to us of the next act of Judas—that of receiving the promised reward, though from the related fact that he had it the next day, it is certain that he must have received it, but whether that night immediately after the arrest or the next morning, it is not necessary to enquire; but whenever he received it, its possession did not long give him pleasure. The next day, when he saw the enemies of Jesus were likely to succeed in taking his life, he became conscious of the extreme wickedness of his act; he repented of it; the satisfaction of the possession of the thirty pieces of silver was gone. The traitor went to the chief priests and elders and confessed that he had betrayed an innocent person. They made the unfeeling reply to him : " What *is that* to us? See thou *to that.*" He threw down the silver in the temple and went and hanged himself. And as if to make his death appear more terrible and revolting, St. Peter states, in his speech before the council which elected Matthias as the successor of Judas, [Acts i, 16—20,] that his body fell "headlong, he burst asunder in the midst, and all his bowels gushed out."

Judas seemed to have had such a sense of the enormity of his sin that he had no hope of pardon; he did not wish to see the end of the affair, and, perhaps, thought that the suicidal act, together with the giving back the money would release him from the consequences of his treason—or at least modify them in a degree. The other mention of this man in the scriptures, lead us to suppose that he had commited that sin of which Jesus taught that it hath never forgiveness, but is in danger of eternal damnation. [Heb. x, 26, 27]. It seems to be a fact that, wherever the gospel has been known, Judas Iscariot is the person whose memory is held in the most severe execration. [See Matt. xxvi, 24.]

The sin of Judas was, to make an exact definition, the offering for a money consideration, to assist those who were seeking to destroy Jesus, Whom he knew to be a good man from His kind and charitable deeds, a holy man from His stern rebukes of sin and wickedness, a wise man from His wonderful instructions, and a powful Being from the miracles He performed, and which He enabled himself and his fellow disciples to perform in His name, and in doing this to act in the character of a zealous friend.

In II Samuel, [xv, 31; xvi, 20-23; xvii, 1-2, 21-23]. mention is made of the counsel and acts of Ahithophel, who had been a trusted counselor to King David (an office something like an attorney-general in this nation); but he had changed his fealty and essayed to be counselor to David's son Absalom, who had risen in revolt against his father. Because his counsel was rejected by Absalom, and he saw nothing but ruin and disgrace as the future of his life, he went and hanged himself; of whom David wrote in psalm cix, 7—20, which is quoted by Peter [Acts i, 16—20,] as a prophecy of the fate of Judas, or, perhaps, was quoted as a precedent by which to guide the action of the first christian council in selecting a successor to Judas in the apostolic office.

ARTICLE XXIV.

PETER.—Matt. xxvi, 69—75; Mark xiv, 66—72; Luke xxii, 54—62; John xviii, 13—27.

ANOTHER of Jesus' chosen Apostles manifested a marked evidence of cowardice, unexpected by himself, though warned of it by his Master. In Matt. xxvi, 31, it is related that Jesus foretold the disciples that they would all be offended on his account, and that in doing it they would be fulfilling a scripture prophecy. [See Zech. xiii, 7.] Peter with his usual forwardness, ventures to make a solemn assertion that he would never be offended. And when further informed that he would deny his Master three times, he was very positive that even if he should be threatened with death, he would not deny the relation which he sustained to Him whom he had acknowledged as the source of eternal life. [See John vi, 68.] There is no reason to doubt that when he made these emphatic declarations, he sincerely intended to be faithful to Jesus.

We notice in St. Luke's account [Luke xxii, 36,] that but a short time before the betrayal Jesus had directed the disciples to buy swords; and Peter had provided himself with one, and not unnaturally, he may have thought that the time had come to use it. At the time of the arrest of Jesus Peter with his sword attacked one of the arresting party, and doubtless would have resisted the officers still further had not Jesus ordered him to put up his sword. In these acts he manifested an earnest desire to be faithful to his Master. He, like the other disciples, thought the Christ's kingdom was to be an earthly one, and rightly

PETER DENYING JESUS.

judged that in order to bring that idea to a success, his servants must fight; and although there were but few of them comparatively, he had great faith in the power of Jesus to accomplish great results with but few followers, as the miracles which He had performed in the presence of many people gave him reasonable proof that He had all the power necessary to accomplish any object which he desired.

Perhaps, had Peter been accosted after the arrest by some one in authority and required to give his testimony in the case, he might have responded affirmatively, and kept his promise; but when, as they were seeking for witnesses, and only a young girl recognized him, and he, not desiring to appear in the case, thought that by denying the fact to her he should escape being called on to testify, told the lie without really designing to forsake his Master at the last. Though a short time before he had forsaken Jesus and fled, he soon turned back and followed at some distance, seemingly determined to be at hand should his assistance be required.

We may suppose that while the proceedings of that eventful night were occurring, the feelings of this disciple were in a very excited state—he was in no condition of mind to remember the warnings and instructions which Jesus had given him and his fellow disciples, his attention being absorbed by the events taking place, with probably fearful forebodings of the result of them in the future, left him no leisure for a calm reflection upon the subject of what action his duty to his Master required of him—all was confusion around him, which caused indecision and perturbation within him. While in this condition another girl saw him, and asserted her suspicion that he was with the accused, which he again denied with a solemn asserveration that he was telling the truth. After a time, in which he had joined in the conversation with those about him, they who stood near became convinced that he was a disciple of Jesus and charged him with it, when in order to keep up a consistency with his former assertions, he began to curse and to swear, declaring that he did not know the man. At this juncture the cock crew, and the Lord turned and looked at the liar and swearer, who was immediately reminded that he had violated his solemn promise; had added falsehood upon falsehoods and imprecated curses on—whom?—it may have been on the young women who had been so inquisitive, or on those about him who were so suspicious of him, but in reality the curses came upon himself—he remembered his falseness and his falsehoods and his impiety, and with feelings of deep anguish he went out and wept bitterly. At the first he was over-confident, and thought he could withstand all opposition in support of his Master; and at the last he was rendered so weak and irresolute by the excitements of the occasion, that he would not acknowledge the truth even to a young girl. His great trial came from an unexpected source. This fact teaches that it is important to watch in all directions for danger.

The xxii chapter of St. Luke's gospel 31st and 32d verses read: "And the Lord said: 'Simon, Simon, behold, Satan hath desired *to have* you, that he may sift *you* as wheat; but I have prayed for thee that thy faith fail not; and when thou art converted, strengthen thy brethren.'" In the Revised Version the same verses read: "Simon, Simon, behold Satan asked to have you that he might sift you as wheat; but I made supplication for thee that thy faith fail not; and do thou when once thou hast turned again stablish thy brethren."

The xvii chapter of St. John's gospel contains a prayer which the Savior prayed, and the 9th to the 24th verses inclusive, is probably the part of it which Jesus referred to in the verses from St. Luke just quoted. He may at some other time have offered a special prayer for Peter, but to my mind the series of petitions reported by St. John, very well answer to the description of a prayer that Peter's "faith fail not," although it included the other apostles.

It is probable that this prayer was the cause of the final return of those, who at the time of Jesus' arrest forsook Him, to their former faith in Him as the Christ, and emboldened them to declare their convictions and argue their plausibility with a wisdom which their opposers were unable to gainsay; so that, as the result of Peter's great sermon on the day of Pentecost, three thousand persons were added to the number of the disciples. [See Acts ii, 41.]

We may learn from the gospels and epistles which have come down to this generation (more than one thousand eight hundred years,) that Jesus is still at the right hand of God making intercession for those who, through the temptations of Satan are led to deny Him or His truths, and if they will repent as Peter did, and return to their allegiance to the Lord who bought them [II Peter ii, 1; I Cor. vi, 20; Acts xx, 28] with His own blood, they will be permitted to see and share in His glory. [See II Cor. iii, 18,] and enter in the rest that remaineth for the people of God. [Heb. iv, 9.]

RT. REV. E. R. WELLES, S. T. D.

THIS PAGE IS DEVOTED

TO THE MEMORY OF THE

RT. REV. EDWARD R. WELLES, S.T.D.,

THIRD BISHOP OF MILWAUKEE.

Born at Waterloo, N. Y., Jan. 10, 1830.
Ordained Deacon at Geneva, N. Y., Dec. 20, 1857.
Ordained Priest at Waterloo, N. Y., Sept. 12, 1858.
Became Rector of Christ Church, Red Wing, Minn., Oct.3, '58.
Consecrated Bishop of Wisconsin,* at New York, Oct. 25, '74.
Died at Waterloo, N. Y., Oct. 20, 1888.
Buried at Milwaukee, Wis., Oct. 24, 1888.

To Bishop Welles' advice and encouragement, seconded by the favorable opinions of several of the leading clergymen of Milwaukee, and the President of the Milwaukee W. C. T. Union, the author of this volume is indebted for deciding to publish at this time, what he supposed would fulfil its mission by being sent out to the public in a christian newspaper. To him and them his thanks are hereby publicly expressed. (See testimonials inside of covers.)

*The name of the Diocese of Wisconsin was changed to Milwaukee in June 1887.

INTRODUCTION TO BISHOP WELLES' SERMON.

IN the preceding articles the subjects have mostly been taken in the order in which they occur in the books of Genesis and Matthew; but when they were completed, there was one parable which seemed to the author the most pertinent one in the gospels for this series of articles, and instead of writing upon it he requested of the Rev. E. S. Welles a sermon by his father on that parable, which request was granted. The sermon is as follows:

THE PENITENTIAL GRACE OF HUMILITY.

THE PRODIGAL SON.

TEXT.—And when he came to himself, he said: . . . . . .
I will arise and go to my father. [Luke xv, 17—18.]

THE Parable of the Prodigal Son, "We might say," says Trench "if it be permitted to compare things divine one with another; call the pearl and crown of the parables of scripture."

It has also received the title of a gospel in the Gospel, and certainly the all-embracing nature of its teachings, the full circle of doctrine it contains would abundantly justify the epithet.

There have been differences of opinion and varied interpretations in regard to its great primary application; but its general teaching the all-important practical lesson it inculcates, no one can overlook who strives to draw from the Word of God precepts and rules for the guidance of daily life.

The parable is a history as well as a gospel—a history of personal experience; a personal appeal to every human life, showing us all the mercy of God towards us, by holding up as in a mirror before us, our own ingratitude and sinfulness.

In the departure of the younger son from home, and the ills which befell him in the "far country" whither he journeyed are typified the certain downward path of the irreligious and the sorrows and sufferings which, sooner or later, inevitably are the results of sinful courses on earth. It teaches us that men cannot lay out their lives for self and pleasure, living independent of God and duty, without realizing in their own experiences of life, the misery of the prodigal—that sense of the barrenness and wretchedness of sin which finds utterance in the words of that great English poet who, with everything that fortune and rank and genius could give him; who with capacities for good all sacrificed to what the world calls pleasure, and before he had reached half the allotted period of man's life, could in the reality of his want, exclaim:

> "My days are in the yellow leaf,
>   The flowers, the fruits of love are gone;
> The worm, the canker and the grief
>   Are mine alone.
>
> The fire that on my bosom preys,
>   Is lone as some volcanic isle;
> The torch is lighted at its blaze—
>   A funeral pile!"

And what a burial of the gifts and graces of God is every life of continuing and wilful sinfulness—the hopes once vital with active energy, now mere skeletons of the past; the resolutions of our better days, sincerely, and it may be prayerfully, cherished, death beneath the weight of sins which were deliberate violations of them, and the good intentions which glowed and burned with life have been long since wasted and trampled, only paving the downward way.

In the word which in our translation is rendered "riotous"—"he wasted his substance with riotous living," the dreadful folly of the sinner is most vividly set forth—ἀσώτος riotous or dissolute is a compound word, and it signifies the life of one who in his wild way of living thinks that he needs not spare—that he will never come to an end of what he has, and it is this terrible delusion that blinds men, when the inordinate lusts of the flesh, or the inordinate love of money, or wilful neglect of the ordinances of God, and entire devotion of soul and body to the world are taking them captive and leading them on to ruin, and when, like the prodigal, they begin to be in want—when in moments of seriousness they realize to some extent their spiritual needs, how often do they try to find relief by plunging deeper into the sinful vortex that is swallowing them up. They entangle themselves more and more in the cares of business.

The wealth—the possessions which they started in life with the idea of accumulating and using as ministers to their pleasures and their wants—these things have been so sought and worshiped that the true end and aim of wealth has been entirely lost sight of, and the man becomes the slave, and gold the master.

They become more and more devoted to the sinful pleasures of the world; and then they find that the joys and delights for which they once had so keen a relish soon grow flat and unpalatable, and the drudgery of Satan's service begins, and the vileness of sin long hidden beneath tempting glosses, and the loathsome dregs of that Circean cup which they thought would always flash as brightly as it did when in an evil night it lured them from the path of right and duty—the vileness and the dregs are forced upon them unwillingly; yet not able to refuse, for these alone can satisfy the cravings and gnawings of their sin-stricken, degenerate nature.

What young man ever thought, when first he turned from living in accordance with the lessons of the bible and the instructions of a christian home, that before many years had been added to his span of life, spiritual darkness would have become an evil power and presence in his soul; he thought that, at the most, a neglect of religious duties would be but a negative evil; but this can never be—for it is a law of our nature that something must fill the heart—must engage the affections of man: truth and its glorious freedom, or lies and their degrading slavery.

In the great battle of life none are spectators—one and all—old or young, must take sides; who are not Christ's freemen are Satan's slaves; and every conflict —every temptation draws more clearly the lines and marks more distinctly the fact that we are committed to one side or the other. Every time we fall under the dominion of sin we become more the slaves of Satan; whenever in God's name and strength we resist the evil one we purchase to ourselves a higher degree in spiritual grace as Christ's freemen. Whenever we wilfully and deliberately sin, or having sinned are content to live impenitent, we are to the extent of our capacity robbing our life of its true life—sacrificing to that which is of the earth—earthy, the grace and the ornament of our immortal being. As fearful as is this end of sin and shame, it is an issue which lies in wait for any and every human being who forgets God and tries to live in and to himself.

This is, in brief, the history which the parable unfolds—a history not less true than sad, as the experience of many human lives bear evidence. And as its history is the history of fallen man, so is its gospel the good news of God to all mankind—the full and free invitation of that blessed Savior who came to earth to call sinners to repentance, entreating all who know the wretchedness of a life apart from God to return to their father's home—to throw themselves on the riches of His mercy and henceforward to live not to the lusts of men but to the will of God.

As the first step in his return to a better life the Holy Spirit awakens in the sinner's heart a desire which is based on man's faith in the unchanging love of God: "I will arise and go to my Father."

The career of sin, as we all well know, is ever carrying man further and further from his God. In his weakness and wickedness he despises the gifts and the privileges of his heavenly sonship; but God neither forgets nor forsakes him. Bitter punishments find out his sins—but they are expressions of His love who ever loves and would ever save the sinner; and it is this severe and loving discipline that often checks the course of the careless and sinful man and brings him to himself.

It was when the younger son came to himself that he said: "I will arise." Deeply significant are these words: "he came to himself," teaching us that coming to ourselves and coming to God are one and the same thing; for He being the true ground of our being when we find ourselves we find Him—or rather, because having felt after in faith and found God, we have truly found ourself." [Trench.]

"But what is it that gives the sinner a sure ground of confidence that, returning to God he shall not be repelled or cast out? It is the adoption of sonship which he received in Christ Jesus at his baptism, and his faith that the gifts and calling of God are on His part without repentance and recall." [Trench.] In baptism he was made a child of God; he has grieved his Father's heart and gone from His presence—but that Father will in no wise cast him out if he in penitence returns. He was made a member of Christ long since; all spiritual life seemed wasted and gone—but the grace of Christ is life-giving; for He is the resurrection and the life. He was made an inheritor of heaven; for years he despised his birthright; but his privileges abide for him—God's grace abides! The gifts of God are without recall—but that man may receive the benefits of this grace he must show his earnest desire by arising and going to his Father and making unto Him full confession of his sins.

The nature of all sin is this: that, whatever may be its effects upon ourselves or others, its great heinousness consists in its being an offense against God. Therefore, the beginning of all true repentance is the earnest conviction of this truth. Until the repentant man, in heartfelt, sincere prayer, humbles himself before God and confesses his own unworthiness: "I have sinned against Heaven and before Thee," he cannot look with any hopefulness for signs of God's mercy and favor and grace.

Surely, when a sinful man would return from that far country of wilful disobedience in which years of his life have passed; when he would return to his Father's home, most carefully should he cherish this just feeling of humility and devotion; "for there is nothing greater in the gifts of the Holy Spirit, nothing more precious in the treasures of God; nothing more holy among all the graces—and when a man would rid himself of his sinful habits and arise and go to his father bringing the tribute of a broken, humble, contrite heart, he will be met while yet a great way off; there will be no severity nor sternness in the infinite loving kindness of Him who would embrace in His arms all the weak and weary and heavy-laden of earth that He might give them rest.

That first feeble realization of his own sinfulness and wretchedness; the first weak motions towards good; the ripening desire to lead a christian life, were whisperings of the Holy Spirit of God, striving with the inner man. He may not feel now as fully as one day he surely will—if he is faithful and earnest in his christian life, the goodness and holiness of Him to whom he is returning; but if only he arises and comes to his father, he will be strengthened in the way, for God will draw him to Him with the tender cords of affection and will shadow his onward path with his great love, that he may be shielded from the evil that is in the world.

But that he may thus meet with evidences of divine love, there must be on his part a full and free confession of sin and an earnest resolution to abandon it, God being his helper, henceforth and forever. He must not seek to hide from the eye of God his own moral loathsomeness, nor must he deceive himself with the idea that the christian profession is a way of life easily attained and easily kept.

It is the blessed privilege of the truly penitent to believe without doubt that, if he sincerely confesses and heartily repents him of his sin, God will, for Christ's sake, forgive him; but though God forgives, man is not to forget his past sinfulness. Repentance does not end with a sense of forgiveness; but rather should forgiveness deepen and strengthen its fervency and its reality. The relation in which repentance and forgiveness stand to each other is set forth in passages such as this from the book of the prophet Ezekiel [xxxvi, 31.] Then [see verses 25—30 paraphrased] after I have cleansed you, after I have given you a new heart, after I have heaped all my richest blessings upon you, "Then" under a sense of these—"shall ye remember your own evil ways, and of your doings that *were* not good, and shall loathe yourselves in your own sight for your iniquities and for your abominations." It is not only so long as he is in suspense concerning the forgiveness of his sins, that the sinner is to exercise repentance—for the more real his knowledge becomes of the forgiving love of God, the stronger is the reason (and he will feel it so,) that he should mourn for ever having sinned against such love.

Let a man feel that in returning to his Father's home he is coming into the presence of a God pure and holy, and yet so merciful that, although he has wasted his substance in riotous living; has worn out years in earthly cares which were given him for heavenly preparation; has made the riches and honors of this world—not the kingdom of God and His righteousness—things first to be sought; brings not the full rich returns of a life of love, devotedness and obedience—but only the gleanings of a vintage pressed into the cup of pleasure; that notwithstanding all this, that father when he sees him yet a great way off, goes forth to meet him and receives him with the kiss of peace and reconciliation, and brings forth the robe and the ring and the shoes as tokens of his full restoration to all the privileges of sonship and inheritance. Let the truly penitent feel that the relation in the parable is but an imperfect type of God's loving kindness, and he need not be exhorted to carry the sorrows of his repentance into the daily thoughts and meditations and prayers of the closet, and day-by-day to show forth in his life an active sense of God's unmerited and abounding goodness. Deep, earnest, life-continuing and self-mortifying penitence is that hidden path along which the Christian walks with his God.

It is not the mere profession of penitence—it is not the hastily uttered expression of belief that comprise the essential acts of godly repentance and true christian faith. The duties of that life of which repentance and faith are the conditions and the beginning, are arduous and life-long, and these daily, hourly duties are such . as most severely try the strength and consistency of christian character. And thus a bishop of the church, when speaking of that long contest with pagan philosophy which issued in the complete triumph Christianity, says: "It was a noble triumph, and it is written on an immortal page, even the souls of men; but we may not say that it was the noblest of the triumphs of the Faith, for there are tears of penitence and lives of holiness. And such tears and such lives there will be ever in the Christian Church."

And in that day when God shall make up his jewels, their souls will be precious in his sight, who in their lives have added to the penitential grace of humility that of faith in Christ, which is the earnest of a holy life; who trusting not in their own merits, but in the mercy of their Savior, have felt and confessed their own unworthiness in the sight of God; but who have never made that feeling the ground of careless confidence or inactive despair—but have found in it the rather a continual incentive to earnest and renewed strivings after godliness of life; that, whereas, being long dead in worldliness and sin, they may show forth in their lives the power of a living faith; having wandered and been lost, they may give evidence in their conduct that they have been found of God.

TESTIMONIALS.

FROM THE RT. REV. E. R. WELLES, LATE BISHOP OF MILWAUKEE.

Diocesan Office, 222 Juneau Ave., Milwaukee, }
March 14, 1888.

I have read a number of the papers prepared by Mr. Rawson, and I regard them as valuable and suggestive, and worthy of general circulation. *E. R. Welles.*

I first saw these papers in September last, and at that time spoke to Mr. Rawson of the advisability of publishing them in a book form. *E. R. W.*

[The testimonial of Bishop Welles relates to all the articles up to Number xix, which were all that were written at the time of his departure for England.]

[The testimonials of the other persons here given relate to all the articles which were printed in the "Christian Statesman," which include all the articles up to number xvi, excepting number xi, which was not published in the "Statesman."]

FROM THE REV. DR. IDE, PASTOR OF GRAND AVE. CONGREGATIONAL CHURCH, MILWAUKEE.

These papers prepared by Mr. Rawson, are thoughtful and will prove useful and instructive to those who read them.

Geo. H. Ide.

FROM THE REV. DR. HERR, PASTOR OF BAPTIST TABERNACLE CHURCH.

Pastor's Study, Milwaukee, Jan. 21st, 1888.

I have examined the Papers of Mr. E. Rawson, and take pleasure in adding my testimony to their merit. The practical lessons drawn from the numerous portions of the Bible, are worthy the thought and study of every lover of truth and righteousness. I trust their publication will meet with the reception they deserve from the reading public. *J. D. Herr, Pastor Bap't Tabernacle.*

FROM THE REV. MR. KEIHLE, PASTOR OF CALVARY PRESBYTERIAN CHURCH, MILWAUKEE.

I have examined the papers prepared by Mr. Rawson, which must have required much labor upon his part. They will surely be interesting and of profit to any one who reads them.

A. A. Keihle.

TESTIMONIALS.

FROM THE REV. THOS. FAGAN, PASTOR OF CHURCH OF IMMACULATE CONCEPTION.

Mr. E. Rawson, Dear Sir—I return you "Intoxication." The ideas it contains are very good, and suited to the times.
       Yours truly, *Thos. Fagan.*

FROM THE REV. MR. BROKAW, PASTOR OF CHURCH OF CHRIST.

       Milwaukee, Wis., Apr. 3d, '88.

I have read some of the chapters written by Elijah Rawson, and think that the advice, if followed, would enable one to overcome in the hour of temptation. *G. L. Brokaw,*
    Pastor Church Christ, 416 *Hanover st.*

FROM THE REV. MR. FREEMAN, PASTOR OF IMMANUEL PRESBYTERIAN CH.

  Immanuel Church, Milwaukee, Wis., June 7th, 1888.

My Dear Mr. Rawson,—I have read these articles with much interest. You have made strong points against that terrible evil which is sapping our national vitality. You have done well to bring out the Scriptural teachings and warnings against the sin of intemperance in every form. Sincerely Yours, *J. N. Freeman.*

FROM MRS. HERR, PRES'T OF WOMEN'S CHRIST'N TEMPERANCE UNION.

Mr. E. Rawson,—I have read your papers with much interest, and think their circulation in some permanent form would prove a desirable addition to temperance literature.

Yours cordially, *Anna M. Herr, Pres. Milwaukee W. C. T. U.*

[The articles written since Bishop Welles' departure for England, have been submitted, at the Bishop's suggestion, to the Rev. Dr. Ashley, of Milwaukee, and the following is his opinion:

My examination of the Articles on the Cases of Intoxication related in the Holy Scriptures, composed and about to be published in a book by Mr. Elijah Rawson, has elicited my respect for his patient and persevering industry; and inspired me with the hope, that the study and labor he has devoted to their preparation may be crowned with such pecuniary returns as they deserve and he may need, and prove as useful to their readers as he has conscientiously striven to make them. *Wm. Bliss Ashley,*
      Canon of All Saints Cathedral.

 Milwaukee, July A. D. 1889.

www.ingramcontent.com/pod-product-compliance
Lightning Source LLC
Chambersburg PA
CBHW030250170426
43202CB00009B/693